TRUE
NORTH

Finding the Essence of Aroostook

Other Books by Islandport Press

Stories of Aroostook
Edited by Kathryn Olmstead

Nine Mile Bridge
By Helen Hamlin

My Life in the Maine Woods
By Annette Jackson

The Cows Are Out!
By Trudy Chambers Price

Old Maine Woman
By Glenna Johnson Smith

Return of Old Maine Woman
By Glenna Johnson Smith

Wild! Weird! Wonderful! Maine
By Earl Brechlin

Evergreens
By John Holyoke

In Maine
By John N. Cole

Backtrack
By V. Paul Reynolds

Available at www.islandportpress.com

TRUE NORTH

Finding the Essence of Aroostook

Kathryn Olmstead

ISLANDPORT PRESS

ISLANDPORT PRESS

Islandport Press
PO Box 10
Yarmouth, Maine 04096
www.islandportpress.com
info@islandportpress.com

ISBN: 978-1-944762-99-5 (print)
ISBN: 978-1-952143-11-3 (ebook)
Library of Congress Control Number: 2020932366
Printed in the USA

Dean Lunt, Publisher
Teresa Lagrange, Book designer

Cover photo by Paul Cyr.
Author photo by Becky Shea / Sha-Lam Photography.

For the people of Northern Maine
who welcomed me so warmly
to this beautiful place
we call home

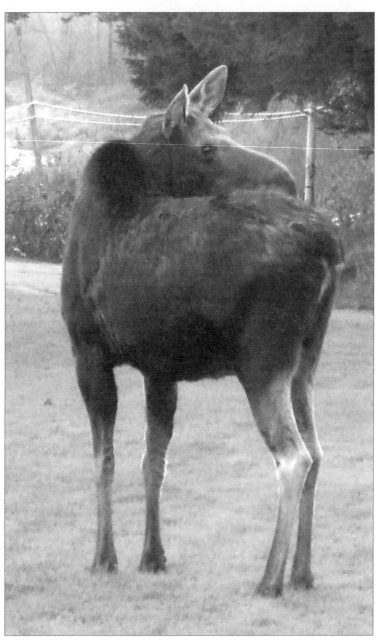

A visitor in my yard.

TABLE OF CONTENTS

The aurora borealis, also known as northern lights, at 4:03 a.m. on March 17, 2013 along the Ginn Road in Presque Isle. Photo by Paul Cyr.

FOREWORD

The columns and essays in *True North* tease out my own fond memories of growing up in Aroostook County—like the aromas of my mémère's kitchen as she fried donuts on her wood cookstove or that time pépère rescued a skunk that stuck its head in a milk bottle.

Kathy's writing captures the diversity and essence of Aroostook's people who are necessarily hardworking and self-reliant because of the remoteness and harsh winters of this far northern Maine land. Mostly the pieces portray how friendly and caring folks here are, willing to help neighbors and others in need at a moment's notice.

Like many born and raised in Aroostook County, I found myself moving away for a better paying job. But I continue to consider it home, and visit and vacation there often.

Kathy did not grow up in Aroostook but established deep roots after moving there in the mid-seventies. She wasn't scared away by the harsh winters and hardscrabble conditions, but rather embraced them, as you'll read when she writes about having to ski from the road to her home or describes the wonderful northern lights she viewed from her outhouse.

I first met Kathy in the late nineties when she was an associate professor of journalism at the University of Maine in Orono and that institution's liaison to the Maine Press Association (MPA). I was an editor at the *Bangor Daily News* and president of the MPA board of directors when we collaborated to read student essays and select winners of MPA journalism scholarships.

We hit it off, in part because of our County connections, and I have considered her a friend ever since. I also enjoyed her work with *Echoes* magazine and when the *Bangor Daily News* was looking for ways to boost circulation in Aroostook in 2010, I approached her to write a column for the *Bangor Daily News* with the caveat that she write about anything she liked as long as it had to do with The County. Kathy readily agreed.

For the next seven years, I thoroughly enjoyed her submissions highlighting the people, places, and events that make Aroostook so special. I also loved the perspective that she brought, looking at the region with such fresh and curious eyes.

True North shares a diverse selection of Kathy's best columns as well as some of her gems from *Echoes*. It is a worthy grouping that paints portraits of County natives from astronaut Jessica Meir to homemaker Ethel Carlson, illustrates the spirit of communities from Allagash to Houlton, and shares in the joy of celebrations from the Acadian Festival to Midsommar.

Reading about moose in the yard, the luminescent night sky, and dealing with where to put all that snow that comes every winter will make many of us reminisce. And while *True North* will inspire pride in those of us who grew up in this region, it also surely will capture the hearts of readers from away.

—Rick Levasseur
Former Editor, *Bangor Daily News*
October 2020

Author's Note
True North: A Fixed Point in a Spinning World

Aroostook County is not just a place in Northern Maine. It is symbolic of rural places throughout the nation that retain the vanishing qualities of life many people long for in today's world. The pace is slow, nature is close, the beauty is breathtaking, and the people are authentic.

When I first moved to Westmanland, Maine, from New Hampshire in 1974, I was impressed by the number of people who had returned to Aroostook County after living elsewhere. As a reporter for Caribou's weekly newspaper, I pursued my curiosity about this phenomenon by interviewing these returnees for a column called "They Came Back." Simultaneously, I worked with young people in Maine's Swedish Colony (New Sweden, Stockholm, Westmanland, and Woodland) to interview elders in their communities and publish three small books about their cultural heritage titled *Silver Birches*. These two projects began years of writing and encouraging others to write about the place in Northern Maine they called home.

I maintained my home and ties in the county after joining the journalism faculty at the University of Maine in 1984. Those ties strengthened in 1988, when Gordon Hammond persuaded me to commute weekly and join him in a publishing venture: *Echoes*—a quarterly magazine portraying the beauty and culture of Aroostook. We worked together until 1995 and I continued producing the magazine from my home in Caribou until 2017. After I retired from teaching in 2009, I also wrote a bi-weekly column for the *Bangor Daily News* about life and people in Aroostook County.

True North contains columns from both publications, for readers who can only imagine a place like Aroostook and for those who savor memories of having lived or visited there. As a transplant, originally from Michigan, I share my introductions to rural life and wildlife, in an attempt to reveal the universal in the particular—the night sky and ice-out, genuine people and their cultural roots, and an intimacy with nature in every season.

Grouped under the headings: Typically Aroostook, Living with Wildlife, High on the Land, Deep Roots, and County People, the essays are impressionistic, reportorial, and often humorous, including a *Bangor Daily News* column on garden slugs that inspired a limerick on National Public Radio's "Wait, Wait, Don't Tell Me." Friends all over the country let me know they had heard it.

The title *True North* describes the quality of life portrayed in these essays—an orienting point, internal or geographic, that keeps you on track in a world sometimes at odds with nature and with basic human goodness. Combined, they affirm that traditional values are still alive in places like Aroostook County, Maine.

—Kathryn Olmstead
Caribou, Maine
October 2020

TRUE NORTH

Finding the Essence of Aroostook

TYPICALLY AROOSTOOK

The Night Sky

The Big Dipper hung low over the highway in front of me as I drove north on Interstate 95. It was one of those crisp, clear evenings when the sky turns deep blue after sunset. I couldn't wait to get to Caribou to examine the night sky from my front yard.

I was not disappointed. The sky was a blanket of stars, bisected by the Milky Way—a broad swath, millions of stars, in an arc over my head.

Every time I experience such an evening, I am struck with wonder at the vastness of the universe and the minuteness of my place in it. I try to imagine something totally beyond my comprehension. I think about my life in a way quite different from my general focus on day-to-day activities.

Observing the firmament provides a periodic perspective on existence that I find valuable. Yet, in recent years, I have come to realize that I am among a dwindling number of people on the East Coast with such a pure view of the heavens.

Students from urban New York, Massachusetts, Connecticut, and Rhode Island at the Job Corps Center in Limestone, twelve miles north of Caribou, saw a truly dark night sky for the first time after they arrived in Aroostook County.

"I was in awe," said Menelike Craig of Brooklyn, recalling his first views of a shooting star, the aurora borealis, and a yellow moon. "I was able to make out the Big Dipper, something I never saw in

The International Space Station joins the stars above Fort Fairfield on February 11, 2011. Photo by Paul Cyr.

my life," he said, explaining that bright light from the city makes it difficult to see the stars.

One of the many gifts of living in Northern Maine is darkness. Satellite images of the East Coast show Maine's north woods as an island of darkness surrounded by patches of light—the largest undeveloped forest east of the Mississippi.

Yet dark nights are becoming rare.

"All living things benefit from natural darkness," says a National Park Service (NPS) flyer on the night sky. "The night sky is everyone's heritage, but light pollution is rapidly eroding the unspoiled view of the stars."

The flyer explains that light pollution is not the inevitable side-effect of progress but is instead indicative of wasteful and inefficient outdoor lighting. Shielded and full-cut-off light fixtures, like those with motion sensors, can reduce unnecessary light, as well as save energy. "Protecting dark skies doesn't mean throwing civilization back into the Dark Ages," according to the NPS. "It simply requires that outdoor lights be used judiciously."

Writer Verlyn Klinkenborg calls our circadian rhythms of waking and sleep fundamental to our being. "Darkness is as essential to our biological welfare, to our internal clockwork, as light itself," he wrote in a July 2013 *National Geographic* article.

"In a very real sense, light pollution causes us to lose sight of our true place in the universe, to forget the scale of our being, which is best measured against the dimensions of a deep night with the Milky Way—the edge of the galaxy—arching overhead."

The first year I lived in Aroostook County, my husband and I skied from the road to our house in the winter, crossing an open field, for about a tenth of a mile. One night on one of those treks, we noticed a bright band of light directly overhead, not the stars of the Milky Way but a solid arc.

An hour or so later, a call to the outhouse brought me back into the yard. The band of light had moved to the north and widened. As time passed, the glow became the dancing luminescence of color that we would witness time after time thereafter—aurora borealis.

I have lived in Aroostook County long enough now that I can hardly imagine the loss I would feel were I unable to wander out into the darkness and be so small.

"I will miss it when I go home," said Brooklyn resident Craig. "You want to be part of it. You don't know what you are missing until it's gone."

Rags, Rugs, and Refuse

When I moved to Maine in 1974, I thought I had stepped back a generation, into a time my mother used to tell me about as she recalled her childhood in rural Illinois.

Only recently had my next-door neighbor, Ethel Carlson, stopped weaving her own rag rugs on the Swedish loom in her corner bedroom. Once clothes were worn out, she would spend evenings cutting them into strips and tying them together for use as the weft on the loom warped with sturdy cotton or linen string.

The life of a rag rug in Ethel's house began in a bedroom or hallway. It moved to the kitchen when it became a little worn, then to the front or back doorway and finally to the shed, where the dog might scratch it into a bed for the night.

In the days before secondhand stores and sanitary landfills, a garment was not discarded just because it was faded, torn, out of style, or outgrown. It had a long tour of duty in the household. The total amount of waste leaving that household was so small it could be accommodated in a family dump someplace on the farm.

I was reminded of Ethel's rag rugs when I read a book by Glenna Johnson Smith of Presque Isle. In *Old Maine Woman: Stories from the Coast to the County,* Smith recalls growing up in Hancock County in the 1920s.

"When a much-patched dress was too worn to wear, Mama saved the buttons, snaps, buckles, and hooks and eyes. Then for future quilts, she cut up any pieces that still held together. In later years she never could understand why people bought new cloth for quilt making. The whole point of quilting was to get something beautiful and warm from discards."

Kathleen Johnson, Glenna's mother, patched and darned white sheets and tablecloths until they were no longer usable. Then she washed and ironed them, cut them into pieces, and packed them away to be used as bandages in an emergency.

"They were really rags before they could be called dust rags," Smith writes. "Once a young family was burned out and Mama's old soft white pieces served for diapers, crib sheets, and handkerchiefs."

She took a cloth bag to the grocery store and her own dish to the butcher and the fish man, so there were no disposable wrappings. Table scraps went to the neighbor's pig or were thrown into a little pit behind the house.

"What the small animals and birds didn't eat became compost. Out of that little pile grew the biggest blackberries in town."

Because Smith's mother grew and canned her own vegetables and pickled and preserved her own fruit and berries, they had few tin cans to discard. Lard and peanut butter came in little tin pails used forever for berry-picking.

"I tell myself, something must have been thrown out," Smith writes of her family home. "Not shoes, because Papa learned to put on soles and heels. Not old pots and pans with holes in them—they could be patched. Not old magazines—they were given to shut-ins. The waste paper was needed to build the three wood fires."

As she watched the garbage truck move from home to home on her street in Presque Isle noisily chewing the week's accumulation of trash, she could imagine her mother's scowl of disapproval. "I can't recall from my childhood in the 1920s that we had any garbage to speak of."

What a difference a generation makes. My years as Ethel and Albin Carlson's neighbor included a stint as editor of the weekly newspaper in Caribou. I could not help but appreciate their thrift as I observed waste disposal become front-page news more often than any other topic.

From sophisticated wastewater treatment plants to fines against potato processors for polluting the river to creation of a new tri-community landfill, waste management was a major expense to the city and its businesses. We wrote features on the city's first "garbologist" and on the first redemption center for bottles and cans. (The idea was new to those who could not remember when milk came in bottles that were sterilized and reused by dairies and farmers.)

Today, more than thirty years later, we are still rediscovering what the Carlsons and the Johnsons did instinctively.

"But they were poor," some say. "They had to conserve; they had no choice."

Do we?

ICE-OUT

When a *New York Times* reporter visited one of my feature writing classes at the University of Maine as a guest speaker, she wondered if my students could give her some information for a story. She wanted to know about a Maine phenomenon called ice-out.

"Lake ice-out or river ice-out?" was the first response from the class. Perplexed, the reporter confessed she had never considered the difference, and proceeded to let the students enlighten her on one of the natural wonders of the north.

The passing of the ice is such a carefully watched, long-anticipated sign of spring, it is duly recorded and celebrated by many observers of lakes and rivers in Northern Maine.

"I so look forward to that milestone of spring because now we know warmer weather is upon us and fiddleheads won't be far behind," said Colleen Murphy of Caribou. Colleen keeps a close eye on the Aroostook River and likes to predict what day the big sheets of ice will flow over the Caribou dam and fill the river between Caribou and Fort Fairfield.

"Word of ice-out spreads fast in a small town and loads of people head for the river's edge to see what they can see," she said of the annual spring ritual. "In some years, when the ice-out is especially dramatic, the roadway will be lined with vehicles with literally hundreds of people watching and socializing."

Fort Kent holds a contest to predict the minute the ice goes out on the Fish River. The person who bought a $2 ticket for 5:11 p.m. in 2009 won $200.

Colleen's brother, Gary Cameron, recalled waiting for ice-out with his father, and "watching tons of ice break over the Caribou dam . . . and grind its way to Canada." It was a time for father and son to just be together and discuss world problems.

At Madawaska Lake, near Stockholm, Stanley Thomas spent forty-one years greeting customers at Stan's Grocery, where he kept a day book recording the dates of ice-out from 1964 to 2005.

"The earliest it went out was April 20," he said. "The latest was May 30, but it was usually right around May 10. I think it's happening earlier now.

"Once the ice breaks away from the shore it can sit there ten days to two weeks," Stan said of the shrinking slab of floating ice. "Some spring mornings there will be a little water around the edge of the lake and by noon it's half gone."

A story is told of a couple who bought an old camp on a lake in Aroostook County. Etched inside a cupboard door was a long list of dates representing decades.

"What's this?" they asked the seller.

"Oh, that's the record of ice-out on the lake each spring."

Fort Kent, on Maine's northern border, holds a contest to see who can predict the exact minute the ice goes out on the Fish River. A string stretches from a flag on a pallet in the middle of the frozen river to an electrical plug on a utility pole on the riverbank that sends power to an old clock in the Fort Kent Block House with numbers that flip to tell the time. When the ice breaks up, the flag moves, the plug releases, and the clock stops, displaying the winning time. Participants buy chances to predict the correct time and the winner shares the proceeds with a local service group, a different group each year. With as many as 1,440 tickets, one for every minute, the contest has raised more than $2,500.

The late Phyllis Hutchins grew up in Fort Fairfield in the 1930s on a farm beside the Aroostook River, just across the border from Canada. She remembered awakening in the night to what "sounded like dozens of big guns." The river had risen and "the deepening, ever-pushing melt water lifted a mile or so of ice enough to break it away from the river banks." The next morning, she watched "a churning, crashing, thundering field of ice chunks push up onto the river bank and tumble down the river."

Phyllis recalled a neighbor family that lost their outhouse to ice-out every year. "At the time, we kids thought that was very bad luck. Now, looking back, I think that was a set-up deal. They rebuilt it back in the same place every year. They guessed it was easier to rebuild than to shovel out."

REWARDS FOR RESILIENCE

When astronaut Jessica Meir spoke from the International Space Station to an assembly of students in Caribou, in October 2019, she exhibited a trait common among Caribou natives who have excelled in their careers.

The valedictorian of Caribou High School's class of 1995, Meir had envisioned herself an astronaut since first grade. When her teacher asked the class to draw what they wanted to be, she drew herself in a space suit standing on the moon. For her high school yearbook, she said her dream was "to take a spacewalk."

In 2009, after years of education and training, Meir was poised to see her dream come true as a finalist for the twentieth class of astronauts chosen by the National Aeronautics and Space Administration (NASA). But she was not selected.

Resigned that her dream would go unfulfilled, she continued her education and research and accepted a position as assistant professor of anesthesia at Harvard Medical School/Massachusetts General Hospital in 2012. Then, in 2013, she was encouraged to apply for the twenty-first class of astronauts at the Johnson Space Center in Houston.

Caribou Middle School student Amelia Godin focused on this moment in Meir's career when given the opportunity to ask a question during the 2019 live chat with the astronaut, projected from the

International Space Station to a screen at the Caribou Performing Arts Center.

"How important was resiliency in helping you to overcome the disappointment of not being selected the first time you applied to NASA?" Godin asked.

"It was very important," Meir responded. "It was a great lesson. You can't give up."

She recalled the heartbreak of coming so close to her dream only to be passed over.

"Do I want to go through that again and have the same thing happen?," she asked herself. "But I knew I had to," she told the Caribou students, adding that she knew she would always question her decision if she did not reapply.

Her resilience paid off. Meir was one of eight candidates selected from more than 6,100 applicants for the 2013 class of astronauts. After six years of intensive training at Johnson Space Center, she left Earth on the Soyuz MS-15 spacecraft from Kazakhstan on Sept. 25, 2019, and boarded the International Space Station 220 miles away seven hours later. On October 18, Meir not only fulfilled her dream, but also made history as a member of the first all-female spacewalk.

"Never be afraid to take a risk and fail," Meir told the Caribou students. "It might even bring you closer to what you want to do."

Meir's words echoed those of two other Caribou natives who defied defeat, tried again, and attained leadership positions even higher than those they originally sought. One wanted to be president of the University of Maine. The other wanted to be governor of Maine.

James H. Page was skeptical when encouraged to seek the presidency of the University of Maine in 2011, but he decided to enter the public arena for the first time. He had left a career in academia

Jessica Meir celebrates *Midsommar* in New Sweden on the lap of her Swedish-born mother Ulla-Britt Meir in the early 1980s.

to return to Maine in 1997 and had served since 2001 as CEO of James Sewall, Co., an engineering consulting firm in Old Town. He could have retained the position after he lost the University of Maine presidency to Paul Ferguson, but his candidacy had kindled a desire to seek an even higher office.

A few months later, in March 2012, Page became the first Maine native appointed chancellor of the University of Maine System and the first chancellor to have graduated from a school in the system, the University of Maine at Fort Kent.

"The first experience gave me the impetus to go after the second," he said. "Without that experience, I would not have thought of or been prepared for the hiring process and work required for the position of chancellor. Being unsuccessful enabled me to be successful."

Susan M. Collins came in third in a four-way race for governor in her first bid for public office in 1994.

"I lost fair and square; it was not a squeaker," Collins recalled. "Were it not for Green Party candidate Jonathan Carter, I would have been dead last."

Having left her position on the staff of US Senator Bill Cohen in Washington, D.C., the campaign left her "flat broke, uninsured and unemployed," she said. "I had lived on my savings for fourteen months and did not have enough money to pay my mortgage. I was facing the indignity of asking my parents for a loan."

Husson College (now Husson University) appointed her executive director of the Center for Family Business and she was happily settled in Bangor when, in 1996, Cohen retired from the US Senate.

Her phone started to ring. People wanted her to run for her former boss' seat. Could she give up a secure job and once again face the possibility of losing and being without an income?

"The decision was a difficult one," she said. "But my parents always said, 'You have no right to complain if you are not willing to get involved.'" So she launched another tough campaign. She defeated Joseph Brennan for Cohen's seat in 1996 and was re-elected in 2002, 2008, and 2014. "Had I not taken the risk of losing, I would not be in the US Senate," she said.

In separate interviews, I asked Page and Collins if there were something in an Aroostook County upbringing that fosters the self-confidence and motivation to defy defeat and try again.

"To be successful in Aroostook County you have to be resilient," Page said. "You have to be creative, be prepared to learn, and have a certain humility in the face of facts."

Collins said, "Aroostook County breeds in you a resilience that helps you come back when you meet an obstacle or adversity. Disappointments and setbacks are part of life. You can't let them make you give up your dream."

When Jessica Meir was inducted into the Caribou High School Hall of Fame in 2016, she told students she could easily have given up and decided not to apply again because she didn't want to be rejected a second time. "Luckily, I stuck to it and persevered. Just in the back of my head, knowing that it was the dream I've had for my entire life, I couldn't not apply. I just wasn't prepared to give up on it yet."

After Meir learned in April 2019 that she would leave Earth for the International Space Station in September and return in the spring of 2020, a *Bangor Daily News* reporter asked what advice she would give to young people in Caribou, or Maine, or the world. "Find that one thing you're really passionate about," she said. "I truly believe that if you're not passionate about something, you won't find success and you won't be happy doing it. So find that passion and work hard to obtain it."

In 2020, *TIME* magazine named Jessica one of the most influential people of the year—another reward for resilience.

Delivering the Magazine

You might think I am crazy, even after I explain, but let me try to respond to the quizzical looks I get when I say I love delivering *Echoes* magazine to all the little stores that line US Route 1 between Allagash and Houlton, and Route 2 between Oakfield and Lincoln. The scenery is splendid in every season, and the people—well, take my round of deliveries in April 2005 for example.

I arrive at *Echoes'* home (River's Bend) in Caribou after the three-hour drive from Orono (home of my day job). A cheerful band of volunteers has prepared enough magazines for me to hit the road immediately. "Prepared" means they have inserted an order envelope into each copy, checked each magazine for defects and placed them into cartons each containing seventy or eighty copies. I load my car with five or six cartons, snack on a few of the homemade goodies the volunteers have spread on the kitchen counter and bid them farewell as they begin their lunch break around the dining room table.

"Guess where I'm headed," I say to Walline at the drive-in window of the bank, where I stop to get some cash before leaving Caribou.

"Up country," she responds.

"Guess what I'm doing."

"Skiing?"

"Nah. What do I *do*?"

"*Echoes!*"

She is prompted by the teller at the next window, and they both admire the cover photos on the copy of the new issue I shove into the tray that delivered my cash.

"Enjoy the day" is not just a rote expression. They know I am embarking on a beautiful drive to the St. John Valley.

On my way out of town, I decide to stop at Monica's Scandinavian Gift Shop. Manager Megan Olson is eager to see her new ad and pleased to be the first store in Caribou to receive the new edition. On to Maine's Swedish Colony. In New Sweden, I take back as many of the previous edition of *Echoes* as I deliver, but Anderson's Store in Stockholm takes extras. Anderson's has attracted some of the coffee-drinking customers who frequented Stan's Grocery on nearby Madawaska Lake until it closed recently. They will enjoy the old photos of Stan's in the new issue.

At St. Peter's Country Store in Cross Lake, near the thoroughfare between Long and Mud lakes, Jules St. Peter shows me a photo of his store in 1898. An enlargement of the small, fragile picture shows the building that still stands next to the store. The business has been in the family for three generations. Jules' daughter, Randi, who works the cash register, makes the fourth, but she's non-committal on a future in the business that has caused her father a lot of stress.

In Fort Kent, only a few copies of the last edition remain at Paradis Shop 'n Save, which usually buys one hundred dollars worth.

"Is anyone here who can write a check for the new *Echoes*?" I ask at the customer service counter.

"I can't write a check, but I can give you cash," the clerk responds.

Up the street at Country Cottage, Priscilla Daigle is recycling fabric flowers into large, multi-colored butterflies. She fumes at the glue gun she uses to attach bright wings to their lacy bodies.

"Let me pay you for the last time and today," she says, disappearing to find the sales slip from the day I delivered three months ago. When she returns to the front counter, she is greeted by a customer looking not for gifts but a place to keep a horse.

"You have a barn," she declares. "Could I use it?"

"Sure, but we'll have to fix the fence," Priscilla responds.

"I'll do that. I have always wanted a horse and just decided I am going to start living the way I want to."

I shop for earrings while they chat, and when I approach the counter, Priscilla admonishes me for getting my ears pierced. "She's old enough to know better," she tells her friend, but agrees the earrings I chose are "my colors."

As I travel north, huge slabs of ice float under the international bridge over the St. John River between Fort Kent and Clair, New Brunswick. At Sue's Market in St. Francis the customer ahead of me says Fraser's Helicopter Service is on stand-by to evacuate residents of Allagash.

"Up at Walker Brook, you can hear the water rushing underneath, but there is a huge ice jam. They say it might be worse than '91. The governor came up here with his big entourage."

Between Sue's and Jandreau's, a mile or so beyond, the ice is packed between the river banks. Jandreau's Store closed down last winter, but I stop anyway because I spot Alva hosing down his car. His wife comes out of the house when she sees me, and we catch up on the news as we always did when I delivered magazines to the store. Today the news is the ice.

"We saw the governor go over in his white plane."

"Plane?"

"Yes. I guess the potholes were so bad they had to fly in," Alva jokes.

Mrs. Jandreau disappears when I bring out my camera, but rejoins the conversation when she is sure the picture-taking is over. For years we have discussed the economy, the future and past of the St. John Valley, and the out-migration of young people.

Jandreaus had a "For Sale" sign in their store window off and on for several years before they finally closed the doors. When Alva sees the photos of Stan's Grocery in the new *Echoes*, he says, "He was lucky to sell." I am tempted to accept their invitation to come into the house and sit down for a chat, but I am anxious to see what's going on upriver.

I can almost coast to the next store on my route.

"So, have you seen the governor yet?" I ask in John's Country Store.

"No, but they came in ahead of him to secure the area."

"Secure the Allagash?"

John just stares back at me.

"So, what can the governor do?"

"Not a thing," he replies. "We had to call Augusta to get the potholes filled."

I should turn around and finish delivering in Fort Kent, Madawaska, and Van Buren, but if an ice jam is big enough to attract the governor, I want to see it. I follow the St. John River to Allagash and cross the Allagash River where it meets the St. John. Rafts of ice are pushing up along the shore, but the water is moving through channels. I hesitate before crossing the new bridge over the St. John River above the Dickey Trading Post, built in 1991 after an ice jam forced people from their homes as the town filled with water. What if this jam breaks and I can't get back?

I cross the bridge, turn onto the Walker Brook Road and cross Black Brook. I am not alone. A couple in a van follows me. We meet big, four-wheel-drive pickups as we churn through ruts of mud in the road along the river. I pull off and decide to turn around. The van continues past me. I decide not to turn around. I follow the van.

Five vehicles are parked along the road and on the drive leading into Walker Brook Park. Others approach from beyond, but this is as far as I am going. I pull on my gum rubber boots and plod through the melting snow toward the shore where men and women are taking pictures and comparing notes about people at risk on the banks beyond. One man is said to be cut off from access to the road, but he says he is not worried.

Giant slabs and mounds of ice are packed tight between the shores. They say it is like this for four miles. The water level has dropped downriver. As it rises behind the ice jam, the community waits. My lens is not wide enough to encompass both the enormity of the individual pieces and the expansiveness of the solid, silent ice. My fellow sightseers and I share our wonder as witnesses to this reminder that humankind is not in charge of everything on earth.

Fortunately, the return trip is downhill and I can slither through the soft spots in the road. It's after 4 p.m. when I pass through Allagash, St. Francis, and St. John to finish what I can of my deliveries. These include the drug store and hospital in Fort Kent and Jes's Foodland in Frenchville. Jes's daughter greets me and shares recollections of past ice jams on the St. John River. I buy some warm baked beans for my supper. Her father's recipe is a well-kept secret even she does not know.

As I head for Long Lake and Gary Babin's Store in St. Agatha, I realize I am going to have to save Madawaska and Van Buren deliveries for another week. Tomorrow I must head back to Orono and deliver to all the stores between Caribou and Lincoln that are open on Sunday (Presque Isle, Fort Fairfield, Easton, Mars Hill, Houlton, Oakfield, Island Falls, and Sherman). If I don't make it to Sherman before it closes at five, I'll stop there on my next trip north, before I cut over to Route 11 to deliver to the grocery and drug stores in Patten.

The driveway at River's Bend that was full of cars when I left five hours ago is empty and the house is silent. The only evidence of the day's activity is three hundred mail bags heaped beside the door, each tagged to carry the *Echoes* magazines they contain to more than 2,700 homes across the nation.

I make a meal from Jes's baked beans and leftover snacks, then load the car with the remaining newsstand cartons for tomorrow's journey south. I hope it's a clear day so I can catch my favorite views of Mount Katahdin.

BLOWOUT

It wasn't a big hole, but it was deep and too close to avoid after I saw it—a black space in the white line marking the road's edge. The right front tire took the round hole squarely with a thud, and the warning light on the dash glowed immediately.

My decision to take Route 11 south from Fort Kent was spontaneous. It was only 1:30 p.m. and I had finished delivering the fall edition of *Echoes* magazine to stores north of our office in Caribou— New Sweden, Madawaska, Fort Kent, St. Francis. If I traveled south on Route 11 and returned to Caribou on Route 1, I might be able to deliver to stores in Patten, Sherman, Island Falls, Oakfield, Houlton, and Mars Hill before dark.

Perhaps I'd even see a moose. After seeing two of the gigantic animals stretched out on the beds of trailers, it would be nice to see one still on its feet.

I had just passed the sign for Hedgehog Mountain when the roar that says "you are about to roll onto your wheel rim" told me to pull off. The rim and center of the wheel were intact, but the tire lay underneath like a wet dishcloth.

OK. I should be able to do this, I tell myself. My friend Francine wouldn't think of calling for help, and she's a tiny little thing.

I dig out the owner's manual and turn to the section titled "Steps to take in an emergency: If you have a flat tire." I move three cartons of magazines from the rear compartment to the back seat and locate the jack, crank, tools, and spare tire.

I lean the compact "donut" tire with the distinctive yellow paint job against the front bumper, in clear view of anyone traveling north—a visual hint that I could use a hand.

"Chock the tires," says the manual. I look for rocks, but settle for hunks of sod, and cram them under the left rear tire.

"Slightly loosen the wheel nuts (one turn)."

Right. I try one, then another. They won't budge. I fiddle with the jack, and finally decide I will have to call AAA.

"Where are you?" asks the AAA lady, after confirming I am not injured and am safely off the roadway. Grateful to hear a voice, since no bars appear on my cellphone, I tell her I am just south of Winterville Plantation, near Hedgehog Mountain. Asked for specifics, I add north of Patten, south of Eagle Lake.

She calls back in a few minutes: "Are you in Masardis? My supervisor says you gave your location with a range of 75 miles." So I did. I was so focused on Patten, I forgot to mention the towns in between.

"No," I assure her. "I am way north of Masardis. North of Ashland. North of Portage Lake."

"Then can I say you are in Winterville?" I say yes, even though I had passed the "Au Revoir" sign, a few miles back. "The closest town is Winterville."

In a few minutes I receive a call from a service station in Fort Kent. Help is on the way. I work on the lug nuts a couple more times, then decide to leave the work to someone else and just wait in the car, reading the owner's manual.

Knowing Aroostook County, I was not surprised when a pickup passed me going north, stopped, and turned around at the first opportunity.

"Not sure I can do much, but I could not just pass without stopping to see if you were OK," says a jovial man from Allagash. I assure him I'm all set, and we chat as I name a few people I have known with his last name. "Yep, we're related," he affirms. I give him the new edition of *Echoes* as a thank-you for stopping and he is on his way.

When a full-length empty logging truck heading north stops and starts to back up, I think, "Oh, no, what if a car comes whipping over the hill ahead of him?" Not to worry. He angles the double-bed trailer neatly across the road and onto the southbound shoulder perfectly aligned with the rear of my car.

I run up to the cab and thank him profusely for all the trouble he took to reach me. "I'm all set," I proclaim. "Someone is coming from Fort Kent."

"Just to change a tire?" He shakes his head, smiling. "I could have done that."

By now, I am truly sorry I had called for help.

The logger has just disappeared when a young man in a sedan slows down in the northbound lane. "Do you need some help here?" he calls out.

"All set," I respond with thanks. "I have talked to a service station in Fort Kent."

AAA calls to see if the driver has arrived. I look at the time on my cellphone. "How could it be 3:30?" I wonder, until I realize the phone is suddenly picking up a signal from Canada which is an hour ahead of Maine time. Still, the predicted wait time has elapsed, and I have dismissed three potential helpers.

Then two cars arrive from opposite directions. A pickup going north turns around and pulls up behind me. A sedan traveling south pulls off the road ahead of my car. The two drivers don't even listen to my story about someone coming from Fort Kent. One handles the jack while the other loosens the wheel nuts.

"Are you together?" I ask.

"Nope," one says. "I'm on my way to work, but can take care of this right quick."

Within minutes, the tire is changed and the damaged one stowed in the back of my car along with the tools. Neither man will accept cash, as they sprint to their vehicles. I run after one then the other offering each a magazine as a thank you.

Now what if the driver ordered by AAA arrives and I'm not to be found? I call the service station and am told he should be there any minute. I wait.

Then AAA calls and offers to notify the station to disregard the call for service. I would like to thank the driver for coming, but decide to let AAA cancel the request. Still, I wait a few minutes, hoping to explain that no sooner had I called for help than five people stopped to offer assistance, all within a half hour. If I had only known.

Well, I should have.

REFUSAL TO COLLAPSE

It was to be the largest implosion in the state of Maine. The building that had served as the heating plant for Loring Air Force Base from 1953 until the base closed in 1994 was expected to collapse in on itself in six seconds on August 13, 2011.

Demolition crews had spent weeks removing hazardous materials, weakening steel support columns so the walls would fall in the right direction, and placing more than the normal number of timed charges because of the building's solid steel construction.

Several hundred people gathered under a tent 1,200 feet from the site, digital and video cameras ready to record history.

The countdown began. Charges detonated 290 pounds of dynamite. Three chimneys fell. Some of the walls gave way. But when the dust cleared, most of the 58-year-old building remained standing. The demolition plan was insufficient to bring down the structure designed to withstand the kinds of hostilities envisioned during the Cold War.

"We think the building was just built very soundly," the operations manager for the demolition company told the crowd waiting for more action that was not to happen.

"I was standing right behind the implosion contractor, whose company placed and wired all the explosives," Carl Flora, president and CEO of the Loring Development Authority (LDA), recalled. "He didn't believe it when the detonated charges failed to collapse the building."

Weeks later, the contractor brought in conventional equipment to take the building down piece by piece.

Why does this event seem symbolic? How often is the resilience of Aroostook County underestimated? Like the defiant heating plant, the inherent grit that characterizes Aroostook County helped give new life to Loring Air Force Base in Limestone.

The County began to imagine itself without Loring in the 1980s. The Department of Defense had included the Strategic Air Command base in Limestone on a list of bases scheduled for massive reductions. Local leaders representing all of the county's resources met to discuss how those resources could be energized to help sustain Aroostook without the base—agriculture, forestry, education, health care, business, finance, economic development. Anticipating a loss generated new possibilities.

With the emergence of the Save Loring Committee, the focus shifted to retaining the base at full strength, an effort that was successful in prolonging the life of Loring for another decade. But those early meetings were a wake-up call to the reality of impermanence. They set the stage for the recovery that had to occur after Loring closed in 1994.

By 2011, Loring Air Force Base had become the Loring Commerce Centre with enterprises that employed 1,200 to 1,300 people and generated a total annual payroll of fifty million dollars. The 142,000-square-foot hospital built in 1988, houses the Defense Finance and Accounting Service, which processes vendor payments, payroll, and accounting for military units in places across the globe.

Ten buildings on the former base became a campus for Job Corps students between the ages of 16 and 24 to train in a range of fields from general business and culinary arts to diesel mechanics. The faculty and staff of 135 includes many central Aroostook teachers who were displaced after the base closed. The 200 to 250 students live in the former enlisted airmen's quarters and use the dining commons, gymnasium, Whispering Pines recreational center, auto body shop, and several other buildings.

When the base closed in 1994, Art and Gary Cleaves, Maine National Guardsmen from Caribou, had a brainstorm—why not use buildings and equipment left behind by the Air Force to retrofit and rebuild military ground equipment? They convinced the National Guard Bureau to let them test the idea using two buildings and 20 employees. Within two years, the Maine Military Authority (MMA) occupied about 440,000 square feet in nine buildings and employed between 150 and 200 people.

"With our agricultural heritage, everybody knows how to fix something. People in Aroostook County have that quality as second nature," Flora said.

When United States troops were deployed in Afghanistan and Iraq, the MMA filled the Army's need for increased vehicle repair services. Trucks and rail cars loaded with military Humvees, Howitzer tanks, five-ton trucks, communications equipment, mobile kitchen units, and even field laundries moved on Maine highways and railroads delivering their cargo to an eight-acre compound on the former base to be rebuilt by local mechanics and auto body experts. It was the perfect enterprise for Aroostook County. Later the MMA shifted from military equipment to rebuilding school buses, municipal construction vehicles and firetrucks for a short time, and eventually ceased operation.

It isn't easy to attract businesses to Northern Maine, but Flora said existing buildings and an available trained work force are real assets. "We have a work force with skills and motivation," he said.

Like the steel columns and beams of the old Loring heating plant, the ingenuity and quality of the Aroostook County work force provided the internal strength to create a future for Loring Air Force Base.

MADE TO LAST

When I returned to Caribou after a week away I discovered my chest freezer had stopped operating. It's an old six-foot-long International Harvester that must have been installed when the house was renovated in 1950 because there is no way to remove it from the cellar. It is one of two appliances in the house that is more than fifty years old.

When I bought the house in 1992, I was warned not to disconnect the freezer or it would never work again. But two years ago, it had to be unplugged to replace the outlet. As predicted, it stopped running, and I tried to imagine the process and cost of carving the thing up to remove it.

On the off chance the freezer might have a future, I called the appliance repair shop in Caribou. Wayne Damboise saved me. This skilled technician worked several hours, replacing a relay and ten connections to get the motor running again.

So, I called Connor Appliance Repair again, after discarding the warm food and bailing the water out of the idle freezer.

"Are you sure you want to put more money into that old thing," asked Cindy Damboise, who took the call.

"Well, could we just see what it would take?" I responded.

This time Wayne worked less than thirty minutes and the freezer was humming again. I call him my magician.

I knew he could do it. A couple of years ago he replaced the baking element in my General Electric kitchen stove that previous owners of the house acquired in the 1960s, when Caribou High School replaced the appliances in the home economics classrooms.

Wayne explained the schools had a deal with Maine Public Service, which then supplied electricity to Northern Maine. Every few years, the schools replaced appliances, like the 1962 stove I am still using, and residents could buy them, nearly new, at reasonable prices.

I once thought I would replace this range, but could not find one with a second smaller oven that I liked. Besides, it still works. In fact it holds the heat so long that a friend, staying in the house while I was away, worried that the stove had not turned off and shut it off at the electrical box until it cooled down.

"These self-cleaning models had to be super-insulated because they cleaned at 900 degrees," Wayne explained. "You're cremating whatever is in there."

I remarked on how easy it is to clean under the burners and inside the stove. Surfaces look like new with a minimum of elbow grease.

Wayne said the porcelain on early models was layered on through a dipping process. Since the process caused pollution, manufacturers replaced dipping with spraying. New surfaces are not as thick as old ones, even though they could be with more layers of spray.

The longevity of my freezer and stove made me wonder when manufacturers stopped making products that would last for decades. When did they discover it made business sense to limit the life of their products, so consumers would have to replace them more frequently? When did they adopt the policy of "planned obsolescence"—designing a product with an artificially limited life so it will become unfashionable or no longer useful after a certain period of time?

Adam Hadhazy, in a June 2016 article on the BBC website, traces this strategy back to the 1920s, when light bulb manufacturers worldwide colluded to artificially reduce the lifetime of bulbs from decades to 1,000 hours.

Early incandescent bulbs used carbon filaments eight times thicker and more durable than thin, metal wires in later bulbs. One such bulb, the Centennial Light Bulb, still glows, after 115 years, in a fire station in Livermore, California. (You can see it on YouTube.)

Auto manufacturers also saw the light in the 1920s. Facing competition from Ford Motor Company, General Motors introduced a new concept to entice customers to replace their vehicles early—new models every year.

"It was a model for all industry," writes Giles Slade, author of the book *Made to Break: Technology and Obsolescence in America, a history of the strategy and its consequences.* The strategy generated long-term sales volume by reducing the time between repeat purchases. With the obsolescence of a product built into it from its conception, a consumer feels a need to purchase new products as replacements.

Anyone who has purchased a computer or a cell phone or a printer knows the feeling. There are no magicians out there for these products, and don't even think about the environmental impact of throwing them away.

The refrigerator in my summer cottage on the coast seems even older than the appliances in Caribou. Its freezer is a small aluminum box about a foot square hanging over the right side of the top shelf. It freezes ice cubes, but not ice cream. I don't remember such a model in our home when I was a child, and I'm older than fifty.

When I mentioned replacing it, the man who serves as my magician for the cottage protested. A modern fridge would ruin the

Victorian character of the house, he claimed, and proceeded to sand down and repaint the old Coldspot so it looks like new.

What can I say? It works.

Living
with Wildlife

ALONE?

It is cold, almost midnight. I carve a chair into the snowbank beside the driveway and line it with the tough wool blanket I carry in the trunk of my car in the winter. Wrapped in my warmest down coat, I take my seat to view this evening's display of northern lights.

The pulsing flares of yellow, then red, then green, in an arc across the northern sky, seem to evoke the cries of the coyotes that echo in the valley below. First one, then a chorus of barks and howls alternate in a pattern that is the perfect accompaniment to nature's performance above.

Originally, I came out to look at the comet that had followed me home on the long drive north to Westmanland, drawing my attention from Interstate 95 to the darkening sky outside the left window of my car. By the time I had unloaded the car, built a fire, and returned to the yard to examine the night sky, aurora borealis had become the main attraction with the comet performing a sideshow.

I lean back, arms outstretched, head resting on the snow. Diminished by their luminous competition, the stars still seem close. Everything seems close. I am enfolded, a part of all that surrounds me.

Beneath the hill that rises behind me, a fox family lives in a den with three entrances. We share the same trails all winter, and when spring arrives, the field beneath this snow becomes a playground for bouncing gray kits that cavort in the grass under close parental supervision.

Mr. Fox as seen from the kitchen window.

In June, moose escape into this field from the black flies in the woods, traipsing through the garden, past the house and up over the back hill into New Sweden. Once, I watched a mother nurse her calf in a clearing visible from the kitchen window where I view the animals that share this land. A portrait of maternal contentment for perhaps half an hour, she suddenly stiffened and led her baby gracefully across the hill back into the woods. The next time I looked out, a black bear was grazing in the clearing.

Seated at the base of the slope, I feel the chill as aurora borealis fades and the coyote calls cease. I roll up my blanket and head in to the warmth of the fire.

Sometimes people ask, "How can you live up on that hill all alone?"

Well, it's hard to explain.

The Moose in My Yard

Wouldn't you know. A moose walks into my front yard and I can't find my camera.

The little case is empty. Where did I put it?

I gaze at the huge animal munching on the leaves of the apple trees outside my kitchen window. I guess I will just have to enjoy watching it.

No. I will use my big single-lens reflex camera that has been idle so long the battery is probably dead. I fish the camera out of its bag and turn it on.

"No card." I dig a memory card out of the bag, plug it in, and move to the dining room window for a better view. The moose slides her mouth along one branch after the other, consuming all the leaves.

I snap a picture. Great! The flash is on. Certainly, I have scared the creature away, but no. She munches on. I turn off the flash, take a couple of shots and try to zoom in. My lens won't focus closer than 55mm and she is way too close for my 300mm lens.

I search again for the little point-and-shoot camera, find it, and switch cameras. This one can zoom closer without changing lenses, but it does not capture what I see when I click it—there is a slight delay.

The moose loves my apple trees so much, it looks like I will have plenty of chances to anticipate its moves . . . if only it weren't behind the branches of the trees. I move to the living room for a better view, but those windows have screens on them. What's this? The

The moose seems drawn back to the apple trees in my yard.

seldom-used door from the living room onto the front porch is open. What a gift. I can sneak outside without making a sound. I creep onto the front porch.

The animal stops munching and ambles across the front yard, then stops and looks back at the apple trees longingly. They seem to be calling her back, but she continues toward the driveway, stopping for a taste of the few leaves left on a birch tree in the corner of the yard.

She is moving slowly down the driveway toward the road when she stops. She seems to be drawn to the beech and maple trees lining the edge of the yard. She easily scales the embankment from the drive back into the yard and starts munching again.

I move from the front porch into the yard, concealing myself behind one apple tree, then another—the one closest to the moose. With her rear end facing me, I can't really get a decent photo, so I just watch. I can hear her munch and occasionally huff.

After what seems like an eternity, she heads back toward the house on the outside edge of the yard. There she cleans off the leaves of my only lilac bush.

I move to the other side of the apple tree and try to kneel down to get a view beneath the branches. She notices, but does not stop munching.

Hmmm. What if she decides to return to the apple trees? She is so docile. She wouldn't harm me, would she?

She starts across the yard between me and the house and I wonder. Then she stops and poses in front of the porch. I decide I don't want to hide any longer. When I move into her view, she picks up her pace and clops across the drive, in front of the garage, but she does not disappear into the trees immediately. She stops at the edge of the woods and studies me quizzically.

"Hello, moose," I say, forgetting my camera. "Thanks for the visit. You are welcome any time."

SQUIRREL RELOCATION

I hadn't thought much about what it means to "Havahart" until faced with the task of finding a new home for the cunning red squirrel rattling around in the trap I had set in my garage. The last time I performed this fall ritual, I drove to the rest area on the Caribou bypass, but I am sure the animals found their way back to my house from there. This time, I have to go farther.

First, I have to separate my dog from the process. I let Lucy, a chocolate Lab, out into the yard before opening the door from the house into the garage. I try not to notice how cute the little squirrel is as I lift the trap into the back of my station wagon.

Fortunately, I had put down the back seat yesterday so I could move storm windows from the barn to the house. There is room for both the Havahart trap and my trash. I can take them both to the dump. I have to move fast. What if the animal gets loose in my car?

I wonder whether the dump forbids live trash. Will I be penalized, denied access for the rest of the year? I will drive past the dump, let the squirrel out, then come back with the empty trap. If asked about it when I pass through the checkpoint, I will know.

I lure the dog back into the house, load the trash into the space between the trap and the front seats and set out for the dump—excuse me—landfill.

Actually, I could set the critter free anywhere along here, I say to myself as we drive along the Aroostook River on the Grimes

Red squirrels give me the eye from the ceiling in my garage.

Road—just as long as the distance is greater than that to the rest area on the bypass. The important thing is to stay away from houses, especially those of friends, and to be sure no one sees me. A riverside release might be nice, I think. He will need a source of water, as well as a substitute for the crab apples he has been stealing from the basket on the porch and storing in boxes in the garage and along the top of the willow wreath hanging by my front door. And while I certainly don't want to irritate neighbors, he will need some shelter comparable to my garage and the crawl space under the eaves of the house.

I hear the squirrel scratching and look in the rearview mirror. There he is, busily trying to unlock the flap that closed behind him a short while ago.

I turn onto the dump road. The broccoli fields are dotted with bright green Porta Potties, white buses and stacks of white cartons on flatbed trailers. I don't see any workers, but head for a deserted stretch of the road to ensure my anonymity.

The squirrel is silent. I no longer can see him in the rearview mirror. He is in a part of the trap obscured by the bags of trash. Or did he get out? Oh, no. I would hear him scrambling around in the trash, wouldn't I? He must be sleeping like a baby, lulled by the vibration of the car—or petrified with fear.

I see a farm road between recently harvested fields devoid of crops and people. I pull in to let my passenger go. I read the bold red letters on a sign with an image of a face with down-turned mouth and eyes and an upheld hand:

DANGER/PELIGRO, PESTICIDES/PESTICIDAS,
KEEP OUT/NO ENTRE

Oh, my gosh! I can't let the little thing out here. It will die. I back out and head up over a hill and down toward a wooded area with spruce trees not unlike those in my yard from which the squirrels jump onto the roof of my house.

He'll like it here, I think. There must be water in this dip. I think we are far enough from those toxic fields.

I wait for a truck loaded with potatoes to roar past. Coast is clear. Not a soul in sight. I get out of the car and raise the hatchback. There he is, secure, waiting. I lift the trap from the car and set it down in the long, wet grass.

"So long, little fella," I say as I lift the confining metal flap. Is he delighted or terrified as he bounces over the clumps of grass toward the woods? At least he is alive, I tell myself. He should be grateful.

But I can't stop feeling he must be lonely, if not frightened, in this strange new environment, separated from his siblings. I must get home quickly and collect them. I will bring them all to this very spot.

THE MINK AND THE MYSTERY

I am sitting coatless on the front porch, catching the last warmth of autumn as I read in the afternoon sun. I had moved my Havahart trap from the garage to the porch after seeing squirrel traffic there, and failed to notice the trap was sprung.

Now I see the flaps are down, but the trap is silent. When I creep over and bend down to look, my chocolate Lab Lucy beats me to the trap.

"SQUALK!"

The ball of fur that had been curled up next to the bait pan is suddenly awake, either frightened or furious, or both. I put the dog in the house and lift the trap out of the shade and into the sun on the edge of the porch.

"SQUALK!" the little animal repeats. I recognize the fur. This critter has to be a mink—a marten or a mink. Too dark for a marten. It's a mink. I know they can be vicious and worry it might come back to bite me if I let it out. No need for the eight-mile trip to the dump road to deposit this catch with my squirrels. I will release it right here in my own woods. It is beautiful.

I take pictures and admire the creature. I go inside and observe it through the window. It licks its back and paws like a cat, curls up and goes back to sleep in the sun. I wish I could keep it, but ponder just how to let it go.

The mink seemed to like it in there.

My friend Cindy arrives. I know she will have some ideas. She lives in the woods. And a bonus—she's a nurse. She will know what to do if the critter bites me. Cindy recommends covering the trap and moving it gently to the edge of the yard near the woods. The towel I find doesn't provide complete cover and makes it difficult to grasp the handle on top of the trap, but I manage to move it from porch to woods' edge. I stand behind the trap and slowly open the flap on the opposite end. No action. The towel conceals the mink from my view. What's it doing in there? It must be confused.

It doesn't want to leave. The trap is silent.

I close the flap and open it again. Cindy stands about twenty feet behind me, at the ready. No action. I tip the trap and set it down. A little head with pointed nose and round dark eyes curls itself over the top of the trap, looks at me and goes back inside. It likes it in there. Now I really want to keep it.

I lift the flap again and rattle the trap. The little critter moves beyond the metal, feels the moist ground and joyfully bounds over the carpet of leaves, a dark shadow among the trees.

I return to the porch and compare the droppings left beneath the trap, where it must have spent the night, to the pictures in my "Scats and Tracks" book. Bingo. A perfect match. And the drawing of the animal duplicates the head that peered over the trap and the shadow that disappeared into the woods—"pointed flat skull with small ears, dark brown with white spots on chin and chest."

I wonder if this small treasure could have anything to do with the two dismembered paws I just found on the trail, or rather that Lucy found, during two different dog walks. I study the book to identify the paws. They look so familiar, but the illustrations show the track, not the paw itself.

I have seen that paw, with its slender "fingers" and sharp nails. The black, wrinkled skin of the pads looks almost human. Then I realize, it is the paw I have seen in a photograph on the cover of my own Aroostook County magazine. My suspicion is confirmed. It is the paw of a raccoon. But who killed it? Can a tiny mink take down a burly raccoon?

I am describing the random paws to a friend at the kitchen table when our eyes catch movement outside the window. Galloping along the edge of the yard about fifteen feet from the house is a long, dark creature. It's not the mink. It is considerably larger, like a fat cat. It could not have fit into my Havahart trap. I take my friend out onto the trail to show her one of the two paws and we see the animal again. (It must be the same one—same size, same color, same gallop.)

Back to the book. Not a mink. Not a marten. It can only be a fisher. Can a fisher take out a raccoon? I read the details: "Larger than a domestic cat, but slender, 7.5 to12 lb., pointed flat skull with small ears . . . dark brown, long bushy tail."

"That's our animal," I think, especially when I read, "scat that frequently contains porcupine quills." Porcupine quills! No wonder that fisher was fat. Compared with a porcupine, that raccoon must have been, well, a piece of cake—except for the feet.

NOCTURNAL VISITOR

At first I think I am being awakened by raindrops on the window. But when I look out, the sky is full of stars. Maybe it's a moth caught under the storm window propped open to let in the cool night air.

I lie back, appreciating the breeze off the river. The light tapping is now scurrying—a mouse in the wall. Clickclickclick, silence. Clickclickclick, silence. It's close to my bed.

I turn on the light. It's 1:15 a.m. Clickclickclick. I get out of bed. It scurries across the floor. I scream. It's not a mouse. It is bigger with a furry gray tail.

Where did it go? I shake the rack of blankets in the corner where it had scurried.

Nothing.

Oh no! Did it go down the hall? If it escaped the bedroom, I'll never find it. I look around upstairs. Listen. Silence. I close all the other storm windows I had propped open. My visitor must have crept into my bedroom over the windowsill from the roof.

I return to the bedroom. Clickclickclick. Thank God, it is still there. I slam the door and pick up a little wicker wastebasket. I shake the blanket rack again. It scurries out. I plop the basket over it, covering the thing with used dental floss and tissues.

Now what? I can hear it scratching under the basket.

A pile of plastic-covered matted photographs rests on the bed in the next bedroom. I select one I don't particularly like. It looks big enough. I slip it under the basket.

The animal scratches.

I run downstairs, open the front door, turn on the porch light and unhitch the spring holding the screen door. I do not want to fumble this maneuver.

I return to the bedroom, slip one hand under the photo mat with my other hand tight on the top (really the bottom) of the basket. I carefully lift my visitor, carry it down the stairs, and out the front door.

There! Scram! I throw the basket off the porch.

No action. I peer into the basket. It is clinging there—my first good look at the petrified little creature—a gray baby, perhaps an orphan, not yet red like its six elders I recently transported to my favorite squirrel relocation haven on the dump road.

Go. You're free now. Have a nice night.

Slowly it creeps out of the basket into the herb garden and sits there, staring at me looming over it in my nightgown, backlit by the porch light.

I pick up the basket and wait until it slowly makes its way into the front yard where it disappears into the darkness.

It really was cute.

SLUGS PREFER BUD

My battle against slugs in the garden could tarnish my reputation in the community.

Apparently, the slimy creatures, who look like large snails without shells, were breeding in the thick bed of straw that covered the garden last winter and became saturated with a month of rain in May.

So, I raked most of the straw to the edges, making the garden look like a giant 20-foot-by-10-foot nest, and planted new seeds in the gaps between the few sprouts in the rows of beans. Still, as soon as the tender sprouts spread their leaves the slugs turned them into lace.

Then I remembered someone telling me you could catch slugs with beer. I had a few bottles left over from a party in May, so I tried it. Sure enough. The critters crept into the foil pie pans of beer I scattered between the rows of beans and squash plants.

I was willing to give up a few bottles of Corona, but drew the line when I was down to my nice Irish stout. I was going to have to buy beer especially for the slugs. What brand do you suppose they would like?

I didn't want to be stuck with a brand I'd never drink myself, so settled on a six-pack of Molson, because it was on sale at Sleepers for $5.99. Well, they went through that in a week, and I was not about to return to the same store for another six-pack so soon. I imagined the face of the cashier when I explained it was for my slugs.

So, I went to the supermarket and found a forty-ounce bottle of Budweiser for $2.99. Perfect. They loved it. I caught twice as many slugs with Bud as with either Corona or Molson. I actually watched a slug make its way past the seedlings toward a pan of beer.

Now I was curious. Do they really prefer one brand over another? Was I willing to give up some of my imports for an experiment? Would slugs collect in a pie pan of, say, Guinness?

So, I cracked open one of my last two bottles of Guinness, telling myself it never tastes as good out of the bottle as from the tap anyway. I had wanted to use Budweiser as a control, but could not find a forty-ounce bottle in Caribou. (I must have gone all the way to Presque Isle the first time in my search for anonymity.) In Caribou, it was hard to find anything smaller than a twelve-pack of Bud at the supermarket, so I settled for a six-pack of Moosehead.

I poured pools of Guinness into three pie pans and Moosehead into three pie pans. There was a little left in each bottle, so I emptied them both into a seventh pan—not really a black-and-tan, but close.

The next morning there were two slugs in the Guinness, two in the Moosehead and none in the pan with a blend. Clearly, they had no preference for Irish or Canadian brew, or Mexican if I included last week's Corona. But compared to the number of slugs I found in the Budweiser, this performance was, well, sluggish.

I had to confirm my slugs' loyalty to American beer. Of course, I wondered whether it was just Budweiser they loved or whether any American beer would do. Back to Presque Isle for that $2.99 bottle of Bud and, unable to find an equivalent bargain in another brand, a six-pack of Rolling Rock.

In what had become a twilight ritual, I headed for the vegetable garden, a bottle of beer in each hand, and filled three pie pans with one brand, three with the other. I also placed a pan of each brand in a separate salad garden where smaller slugs feed on the arugula.

The next morning in the vegetable garden I found seven slugs passed out in the pans of Bud, none in the Rolling Rock, a preference confirmed by the slugs in the salad garden where the pan of Bud was loaded with little slugs while only one floated in the Rolling Rock.

I can honestly say I have never bought so much beer in such a short span of time, nor been so conscious of the prices. And, while I was able to scatter my purchases among a variety of grocery stores, I use only one recycling center, so my reputation might suffer when I return the empties.

Meanwhile, I wonder if there is a gardener across the border who would like the leftover Moosehead and Rolling Rock to test the patriotism of Canadian slugs.

High on the Land

SNOWBOUND

It is 9 a.m., Saturday, February 12, 2000. Heating oil prices are so high, I decided to fire up the wood furnace as well as the parlor stove for the weekend since I will be home to feed both fires. I am pleased I replenished my wood supply last spring, but wonder whether I should save it for even worse times. It's a finesse, like farmers who hold onto their potatoes when prices begin to rise, hoping they will go higher. Should I conserve on firewood or use it?

The sun on the snow outside the window beckons me to ski or snowshoe to the top of the hill behind the house, but the wind whipping up little flurries in front of the garage tempers my drive to get outside. Wind-swept snow has erased my ski trail across the field, so I will have to imagine where it was, remembering how it aligned with certain trees on the landscape, much as a sailor uses landmarks when dropping anchor. Sometimes I can see a hint of the packed trail in the wake of the wind, and I know when my foot leaves it because I sink six to eight inches into the snow.

Before I ski I should scoop the drifts away from the garage door and push them as far down the driveway as I can because the man who plows my drive with his pickup has no place to put the snow around the entrance to the garage. If I clear a space for him by hand, he can back up to the garage door and push the snow away from the house.

He told me last week that it was time for me to call someone with a front-end loader to come in and push back the banks to enlarge the space to turn around in the driveway. The plow on the front of his pickup can build them only so high by pushing the snow. Then the banks need a bucket-loader that can pile the snow higher.

"One or two more storms," he warned, "and I won't have space for the snow." So I called the two local people he suggested. Neither could help me, but both suggested I call a family in nearby Woodland. They can come out when their loaders are done working other jobs. I think they will make it before the drive closes in, but I am ambivalent.

Early last spring, I decided it was time to strengthen my independence. This was the year I would buy a tractor with a bush hog for mowing fields and trails and a snow blower to eliminate the snowbanks and the problem of creating space for them.

"I want to be able to mow and blow," I announced firmly to various equipment dealers in Caribou and Presque Isle, describing the terrain of my land and the nature of my driveway. "I want a diesel-powered four-wheel drive with at least twenty horsepower and a cab for winter snow-blowing."

I coveted my neighbor's Belarus and told her so. She praised the independence it gave her, explained how easy it was to operate summer and winter, and told me who to call. Her tractor was too big for my garage, but the dealer had a smaller one, complete with bush hog and blower. I took pictures of it and sent them to my friends. This was it. I couldn't wait. Another neighbor across the road said I could house it in her garage if it didn't fit in mine and we could share the use of it.

But I couldn't make a decision until I had considered all the options. The Belarus dealer thought I would prefer a Steiner and sent me to visit a man who was happy he owned one. The mechanic who maintained my car suggested I talk to the New Holland (Ford) dealer in Caribou, who said he also might have a used Kubota I could look at in a few weeks. My neighbor two doors away said the John Deere dealer had just gotten a used compact on trade, so I went over to Presque Isle and drove it around the parking lot for a while. The New Holland dealer even lent me a new compact tractor to try out for as long as it took to get comfortable operating it (almost three months).

In this sabbatical year from the university dedicated to creative activities and academic research, I have become conversant on the merits of the three-point-hitch; power take-off mechanisms; hydrostatic transmission versus gear shifts; agricultural, turf and industrial tires, and front-mounted versus rear-mounted implements.

I went from the Belarus to the Steiner to the New Holland to the John Deere, back to the New Holland, then back to the Belarus and back to the New Holland again. Then eighteen inches of snow fell on Westmanland and my next-door neighbor came chugging up the hill on his Massey-Ferguson during the blizzard to blow out my driveway. He let me operate his prized tractor, which made me wonder whether I needed more than a compact. Each time a decision was near, another friend would introduce new ideas, and I would gladly delay the commitment.

I tell myself it is the cost or my indecisiveness that has prolonged the purchase of my tractor, but I think it is something else. When I know I cannot get out of my driveway in the morning, life slows down. Expectations lift. I am free.

As the snow falls, the world grows quiet. One life stops and another kicks in. I learn of the cancellations and I get happy. I change my schedule, and the revision is always appealing—reading, writing, skiing, snowshoeing, cooking, even housework seems attractive. Things that have been put off get done, one at a time.

If a blizzard starts when I am in town and I wonder if I will be able to get in when I return home, I let out a whoop as I roll into the garage because someone else has opened up my driveway. I grab an armload of firewood and, once I am in, I feel safe, cozy, content. Let it snow.

I build a fire, select a book or magazine to read, prepare a nice meal, pour a glass of red wine, and settle in, turning on the yard lights from time to time to watch the flakes blow in front of them. Silence is broken only by the sound of the wind, the fire and the cat purring. Peace.

But what if the plow breaks down and I am truly snowbound? Won't I wish I had that tractor with the enclosed, heated cab with front and rear windshield wipers, hydrostatic transmission, cruise control, and power take-off to blow the snow into the tree-tops?

Sometimes it's hard to say yes.

High on the Land

August 5, 2000. Millie has been in the family almost six months. Friends who endured the agony of my decision-making received photos of her on cards, which read: "Announcing the arrival of Millie, The New Millennium Tractor, February 18, 2000, 1,535 pounds, Westmanland, Maine."

She has helped me clear snow from the driveway and till the garden, but today I observed the ethic of being a tractor owner.

"Is that thing broken," a neighbor asked, casting a glance at Millie as he passed through the garage.

"No."

"Then why haven't you mowed any of the fields around your house?"

Well, in fact, I made my debut with the mower behind the house, not visible from the road, but the question touched a nerve.

Today is one of those spectacular Aroostook County summer days—cool breezes, warm sun, blue skies with regiments of clouds marching toward the horizon. When I first moved to Northern Maine, I promised myself I would not stay inside on a day like today.

With a tractor in the garage, the obligation to get out is even stronger. Whatever is on the to-do list becomes subordinate to savoring summer. Forget the textbooks to be read, the syllabi to be prepared, the magazine to be laid out before Monday. Seize this day.

The grass is crisp. The wildflowers have passed their prime. (I couldn't mow down a field of smiling daisies and buttercups.) I define one section to begin with by mowing around it. By mistake, I create a wide swath at one end of the section that turns out to be just what I need for turning space, so I can head straight across the field in straight lines. I create a duplicate swath at the opposite end of my section. Neat. Anyone riding by might think I knew what I was doing.

I would never have dreamed this field was so uneven. There are bumps and mounds and holes invisible to the eye and undetected by the foot. A legacy of the farmer who last tilled here, the ridges running east and west cause my mower blades to lift, then scrape, marring the perfection of my paths, as I mow north and south. Previous to my mowing, I knew this field as a gentle slope. Now I know exactly where the grade changes and when to beware of the drop-offs.

I start small. After an hour of mowing I estimate it will take about five hours to mow the whole field. The sun warms my face and legs as I ride toward it. When I turn north, a cool breeze sweeps the perspiration from my brow as the view of Madawaska Lake ahead takes my breath away, for a moment. Grasshoppers fly out in all directions and two fat gray mice scurry for protection, their hiding places suddenly exposed. Bugs I have never seen before land on my arms and legs. Some of them bite. I wonder if they are special bugs that appear only when people on loud tractors destroy their homes.

I am amazed at the varieties of vegetation I encounter and wonder what conditions create the differences—soil, light, drainage, prior planting. What could cause one part of the field to be a tangle of vetch and strawberries, while right next to it is a stretch of fine timothy, its slender spikes shoulder-high? Of course, there must be ledge beneath the high side of the field where spindly furry-stemmed flowers emerge from a carpet of moss.

I look ahead. Mowing is planning. How am I going to negotiate that spruce tree? How close can I get without being knocked off the tractor by a limb? Can I get between those two trees and still make the turn? How can I maximize efficiency, cutting all the time without traveling over land I've already cut? How can I economize on fuel by lengthening downhill passes and shortening the up-hills? I have been dying to clear a fairly flat, overgrown spot of the field, but not before I walk through it to be sure no rocks are hiding beneath the thicket of red osier and raspberries.

I am not ashamed of my inexperience. I am exhilarated by the opportunity to learn and appreciative of the neighbors willing to take time to teach. I knew when I noticed a nut on the mower hitch touching the wheel on turns that something on the opposite side probably needed tightening, but I didn't know how to do it, nor how to test when it was done. I took a walk to the neighbor two houses down the road and left a note when I found the house empty. On my way home, I spotted my next-door neighbor installing a new belt on his car. He agreed to come up "in a flash," and he quickly remedied the problem.

I am also no longer embarrassed by my new fuel tank. I actually tried to hide it with a pallet when it was hardly used, but now I am more than pleased to be able to pump Millie full of diesel when she gets hungry without having to leave the dooryard. I know just how many pulls on the handle will fill her tank.

I have forty-five minutes before I have to stop mowing and get ready to go out to dinner. I just have to finish this field first. It might rain tomorrow, and who knows when conditions will be this good again . . . on a weekend? I don't want people to see an unfinished

Stora Heda (Big Meadow), my home in Westmanland from 1973 to 2007.

field when they drive by the farm. I apply all I have learned about efficiency and grade and turns. I warn the grasshoppers and mice (they are brown at this end of the field) and suppress my sentiment about the surviving yarrow standing tall in my path.

I am high on the land. My view encompasses the hills along Route 11, miles west of here, as well as the lake and the valley below me. I stretch, on a constant lookout for rocks, as Millie encircles the last section to be mowed.

I ask myself, "What am I doing here?" and realize it is not a rational choice. I think about the distant cousin in England who took me and my sister on a tour of her farm. She was in her fifties when she started farming. Of course, her father farmed, as did her great-great-grandfather, who was also my great-great-grandfather.

Fifteen minutes until dinner. I make my last turn at the top of the hill and *Yes!* The last strip of grass before me is just the width of my mower blade.

BACK TO THE LAND

I was afraid I had fallen off the sustainability wagon, but I have read a book that gives me hope for recovery.

I moved to Maine in the 1970s to learn from the land and from the people who knew the land. My then husband had left a job as a computer systems engineer for IBM, never again to be reminded his sideburns were too long for an employee of that company. We had spent two years as resident parents for the A Better Chance (ABC) program in Concord, New Hampshire, living with fourteen college-bound African-American, Puerto Rican, and Native American high school students from urban areas and the rural South. I was teaching English and journalism at Concord High School, serving as an advisor for the ABC students.

As our awareness of the effects of excessive consumption in our society deepened, we were inspired by Helen and Scott Nearing and other back-to-the-land pioneers to buy an abandoned farm in Aroostook County and learn what we needed to know to live with less.

"An economy based on continuous growth cannot exist forever," we predicted, and when it crumbled, we wanted to be ready.

So we put our belongings in storage, left Concord and set about learning how to grow and preserve our own food, heat with wood, pump our water by hand, live without electricity or telephone, and convert a deteriorating farmhouse into a home.

The outhouse had a lovely window and a view of Madawaska Lake.

We took off the porch to let more light into the house and used the boards to build an outhouse with a lovely window and a door that opened onto a view of Madawaska Lake and the hills surrounding it.

We laughed when the wind was just right and blew the toilet paper up over your head when you dropped it in the hole.

In the summer, we bathed in the lake and showered by dowsing each other with buckets of icy water pumped from the well. In the winter, bathing supplies were always in the car, should knowing friends and neighbors invite us to use their facilities. When the driveway filled with snow, we parked beside the road and snowshoed or skied to the house, toting what we couldn't carry on a toboggan.

Gradually, our commitment to this lifestyle eroded. We could not continue to let neighbors snowshoe in with messages, so we got a telephone. We had to have electricity because we wanted to develop film and print photos. We still pumped water, though, and carried it up to the windowless darkroom that would become a bathroom. Plumbing came last, but a Clivus Multrum composting toilet made the concession to convenience more palatable.

I continued to garden after an amicable divorce left me alone on the farm. But the change from part-time work as a *Bangor Daily News* correspondent and substitute teacher to full-time at Caribou's weekly newspaper and later in the district office of a Maine US Senator left less and less time for growing and harvesting vegetables.

When I took a job in Orono at the University of Maine, my gardening days ended. I began to buy things I once grew. I was seduced by a home warmed without splitting wood or building a fire—just touching a thermostat. Even worse, unable to wean myself from Aroostook County, I ended up traveling back and forth, increasing my carbon footprint exponentially.

As the predicted collapse unfolded, along with unforeseen environmental changes, I was far from the alternative life envisioned in the 1970s.

Enter Jim Merkel, author of *Radical Simplicity: Small Footprints on a Finite Earth*. After reading this book and talking to Jim, I am hopeful it is not too late to begin my own rehab program. Merkel gives substance to the charge, "Think globally, act locally."

For more than twenty years, he lived on the global average income—$5,000 a year. He and his family thrived on fresh, local food and used bicycles as a preferred form of transportation. His speeches, workshops, and his book, gave people the tools to calculate and reduce the amount of Earth required to support their lives.

"It is possible to live as a global citizen," Merkel said in an interview. "Simpler lives help with societal changes."

Merkel, a "recovering engineer," was designing and selling top-secret military computer equipment to arms dealers worldwide when the 1989 Exxon Valdez disaster startled him into a new life based on his awareness of the connection between oil and destructive consumption.

"I knew the truth: fossil fuels are part of every item I consume," he wrote. "Of course, the entire industrialized world stood indicted beside me . . . but in that moment, all I knew was that I, personally, needed to step forward and own up to the damage."

He committed himself to shrinking his own ecological footprint and encouraging people like me to make the changes necessary to live in harmony with nature and with other cultures in the world.

"A lot of people want their lives to be part of making the world better," he said. "The time was never better for deeper changes."

Of course, I am one of those people, and my new garden plot is ready for the seeds I'll buy this week.

BARN BURIAL

We buried the barn this week. Logic prevailed and a decaying structure overgrown with raspberries and redbush became a landscape.

It was an eyesore, a liability, inaccessible. Still, I could only imagine what the excavator and bulldozer would unearth as they scraped away twenty years of growth. I could have spent hours sifting through the debris, but I am told time is money, so I went to town.

Four hours later, I visited the site. The machines were resting. An ancient potato planter and an octopus-like crop duster from the days before chemical sprayers sat perched on top of a couple of huge foundation rocks, symbols of the era that was being buried. Perhaps they should have gone into the hole with the other relics, but I happened in.

The equipment operators attached and reattached heavy chains to the old machines until the arm of the excavator could lift and carry them, dangling and dropping parts en route to what would become my graveyard of old farm equipment.

What is it in me that says, "No, don't bury these objects," even though they are of no possible use to anyone—even though they will only continue to rust and frustrate the mower? Is it respect for those who used them or a deeper desire for immortality?

There was a blacksmith shop on the adjacent farm. The forge still rests among the poplars and brambles. I pick up pieces of wagons and harrows that were probably forged in that spot. Some parts are ornate, curled just so—no more efficient, I suppose, but nice.

I try to piece together the tasks and ingenuity required to make this farm run before heavy machines and easy access to town for parts and service. I wonder at the labor of the horses and men who built this barn, moving monstrous rocks into place, just so, to make a foundation that lasted a century. What will our descendants think of the concrete and cinder block we leave behind.? Will they admire the artistry and wisdom we see in the arrangement of these foundation stones?

I ask the crew to save some of those rocks—to set them aside and move them into a row where the barn wall once stood on top of them. It takes hours, but time is more than money, and the new wall of rocks stretching toward the horizon honors the labor they represent and the history buried beneath them.

Burying the barn helped me accept impermanence—to recognize that one day everything we do or create will be just a memory, and that's OK. Because we are temporary and know it, we can appreciate the value of the present and the beauty of the landscape that shaped the lives of those before us and those who will follow.

SEEDS NEED LOVE

If seeds must be planted with love in order to thrive, my garden is at risk.

Some people can't wait to get out and dig in the dirt as soon as the frost leaves the ground. Not me.

"I'll spend one hour in the garden," I told myself on the sunny day in May I had determined would be planting day. My dog, who retreats when I talk to myself, hovered at the edge of the yard, a safe distance from my grumbling.

Having spent last summer under sheets of black plastic to retard weed growth, the small garden plot was covered with straw in the fall and a layer of manure this spring.

"All you do is scratch away the straw to make a row," said my experienced gardener friend. Well, the straw was packed hard and the dirt beneath didn't look that great. Nonetheless, I raked a few rows with a little hand tool, sprinkled carrot seeds, poked in beans and covered the rows with handfuls of manure and straw, coating my face with dirt as I swatted black flies with my muddy hands.

I have always planted squash on little hills, but these poor seeds are buried in dirt surrounded by a nest of thatch. Six nests of squash seeds, three rows of beans, one row each of carrots, and spinach and two rows of Italian beans and I was done.

I decided to plant a few rows of arugula, lettuce, and more spinach in a small garden nearer the house. The hour was up. I rewarded myself and my apprehensive dog with a nice long walk.

"You had better do something about that woodchuck living under your garage," my friend warned. So I took the advice of another master gardener.

"Pee in a jar," she said, "then sprinkle it around the woodchuck's hole."

I considered a more direct approach without the jar, but what if someone should drive in? I followed her instructions precisely.

The next day, it didn't just rain, it poured in sheets all day long.

"See," I told yet another gardening friend. "Of course my seeds will rot in the ground. I'm not supposed to be good at summer things, like gardening. I'm a winter person."

It's true. By the time I have finally accepted I can no longer ski, the weeds and invasives can be so thick in my gardens I can't find the flowers.

But flowers are not as important as vegetables. This is the year to get back into vegetables. I must improve my attitude, so this little garden will grow. My life could depend on it.

A week passed. We in Aroostook County are congratulating ourselves on living in a place that might have severe winters but not the violent tornadoes wreaking havoc in other parts of the country.

Then at least two twisters touch down in The County, toppling trees, ripping off barn roofs and bringing torrents of rain to gouge huge gullies in the fields and roadsides. I had just read that Mother Nature is beginning to fight back against our destruction of Earth—that earthquakes, tsunamis, floods, and hurricanes are not just happening more frequently by chance. Her message had even reached Aroostook.

I feared my seeds had drowned.

My friend took pity on me and raked new rows in my little plot so I could replant the garden. This time, I said, I will plant my seeds with affection.

Sprouts had appeared in one of the six nests of squash, so I replanted the remaining five. Beans, carrots . . . what's this? A single sprout in the row of Italian beans? I decided not to disturb this row and the one next to it in case other seeds were germinating beneath the surface.

I drove six tall fiberglass stakes around the perimeter of the bed and measured for fencing. I checked the garden every day. New sprouts appeared only in the rows I did not replant. Should I have left the other rows as well?

I made a trip to Orono and met up with a friend who tried to lure me away from Aroostook onto beautiful new bike trails.

"I gave up vegetable gardening long ago," she said. "In Orono we have a wonderful thing called the farmers market. Come biking."

Well, I have to admit, biking is more like skiing than gardening. But this may be a crucial time for my garden up north. I even have a small sign of success. The woodchuck seems to have disappeared.

At Home in the Woods

The snow is too deep to ski, so I set out on my snowshoes to open up the trails near my home in Caribou. The snowdrifts are up to the windowsills and I look down into the living room as I round the house.

The trail made days ago is a slight depression in the snow, invisible in spots. I fix my eyes on familiar trees, bushes, and openings in the woods in order to stay on the hidden trail. To stray is to sink way over my ankles, even on snowshoes.

I know the fox appreciates these trails. Her fresh paw prints and her skunky scent tell me she has come out to say, "Thank you," but she watches me in secrecy. I can see that she, too, sometimes sinks when she leaves the trodden path.

What's this? A new trail through the hardwoods? The latest snowfall has covered the underbrush creating an opening that did not exist before, allowing me access to unexplored places in the woods. Branches I could not reach in the fall brush my face, even after I knock off hunks of snow with my ski pole.

The second time around my "perimeter trail" and through the woods on connecting loops I reverse direction to flatten the trail evenly, placing the wide toe of my snowshoe into the snow left by its narrow tail on my first trip. Sunlight glistens on the dusting of new flakes and the consistency underfoot changes in the time it takes me to finish all the loops in my trail system. Snow under the tall pines packs quickly. Deeper snow in the fields is soft with unpredictable drifts of firmness.

My chocolate Lab, Lucy, bounds ahead of me in the trail, her frosty face smiling as she races back, then gleefully tunnels and rolls in the snow.

I unzip my jacket, throw back my hood and take off my mittens as warmth inside meets the midday sun on my face. Chickadees flit from branch to branch, their winter call the only sound, but for an occasional whoosh of snow dropping from tree limbs.

Is this world real? How can so many people in the world face danger every day while I absorb this majestic winter landscape in Northern Maine? Am I as safe as I seem among the animals, trees, and birds of my backyard?

How blessed I am to live where I can step from my door into nature and feel at home, among friends, walking on snowshoes two feet above the earth. I breathe in the cold air deeply and pray for those who would consider my world a dream.

I make no tracks down the hill over the open field that was once a garden. When the crust hardens I will want to sail trail-less on my skis across the wide sweeping slope, free to make new tracks with every run.

Maybe tomorrow.

Lucy eyes fox tracks in the snow.

THE DOG KNOWS

It's 7:30 a.m., and I am practicing my Bach for an upcoming piano lesson.

My chocolate Labrador retriever Lucy tiptoes into the living room and sits down close to me behind the piano bench.

Could she be ill? She usually retreats to the farthest reaches of the house when I begin to play the piano.

I stroke her and ask her what's wrong. She is still.

I begin to play again. She does not move. Very unusual.

I stop playing and listen for strange noises that might have driven her to my side for safety. Nothing.

"Do you want to go out?"

I get up and move toward the door. She is all waggy and full of smiles, but when I open the door, she backs away.

"OK. I'll go out with you." We walk down the driveway and back toward the house.

"OK. Time to go in. Come on." I stretch my arm for her to pass in front of me and through the door.

Lucy sits down in the driveway—her way of saying, "No."

I think I get it.

My morning routine is pretty structured during the week: up by 6 a.m.; read and sip coffee until 6:30; exercise until 7; shower and get dressed; practice the piano until 8; then begin work, usually at the computer. Today that would be drafting my column.

But over the weekend, I introduced a new walk into the schedule between times at the piano and the computer. Results of recent lab tests for cholesterol suggest that, until snow covers the ground and I can ski, I simply do not get enough exercise. So I decided to double my time on the trails with Lucy.

But today is a work day. I have a long list of things to do. Do I have time for that extra walk? I stand in the hall weighing the value of walking against the tasks I must complete. Lucy sits in the driveway, making a quiet statement on behalf of my health. She won't even look at me when I call to her.

I take her blaze orange vest out of the closet. Lucy smiles and wags when I return to the yard and adorn her for a short walk. But once we are out on the trail, a longer walk becomes more appealing. I will get that work done, probably with more energy from the extra oxygen in my blood.

How many times have I quoted the statement that people on their deathbeds rarely say they wish they had spent more time at the office? And yet, for me to act on that wisdom, I need a reminder from my dog.

I can't give Lucy all the credit. I have read two books that under-score the message: *How We Die: Reflections on Life's Final Chapter* by Sherwin B. Nuland, M.D. and *Power Foods for the Brain: An Effective 3-Step Plan to Protect Your Mind and Strengthen Your Memory* by Neal D. Barnard, M.D.

Using his personal and professional experiences, Nuland demys-tifies the reality we all must face eventually: death. Barnard delivers new evidence that a plant-based diet can preserve brain functions and reduce the risk of Alzheimer's disease and stroke.

Learning from Nuland more about what happens when we die not only reminds me of the importance of living every day fully, but it also heightens my appreciation of the human anatomy—pumping blood, inflating lungs, replacing cells—the miracle of life.

Barnard reveals that what is good for the heart is good for the brain—that a healthful diet combined with exercise keeps arteries clear and maintains a flow of oxygen to the brain. And Barnard has convinced me that more plants and fewer animals in my diet can enhance that life. But not without exercise.

"It is essential to exercise along with a healthy diet, not in place of it," Barnard says.

Fortunately for me, Lucy knows that.

FROM BOMBS TO BIODIVERSITY

The mission and history of Loring Air Force Base in Limestone are well known in Maine, but, until recently, few people were aware of a top-secret installation next door to the Strategic Air Command (SAC) base that closed in 1994.

Now school buses full of sightseers roll through a once tightly secured gate carrying passengers back into the Cold War era, when, as a passenger on one such trip recalled, "Those of us who grew up in Presque Isle spent a lot of time under our desks."

The group was entering an area east of the base that became the nation's first operational nuclear weapons storage site, according to the book *North River Depot* by John C. Garbinski, who served with the 42nd Bombardment Wing at Loring in the 1980s. Completed in 1952, the site contained barracks, recreational facilities, warehouses, offices, weapon maintenance areas, and a separate fenced-in area that included twenty-seven storage igloos.

Known originally as "North River Depot," the site was designed to look like a village from the air. It was in fact, "a maximum-security storage area for the most advanced weapons of mankind," Garbinski wrote, explaining that the facility was the first of five similar storage sites across the country constructed between 1951 and 1953 "to provide operational storage of the nuclear stockpile and to provide a specific number of weapons to their adjacent SAC bases."

The facility was originally composed of two ordnance storage areas, an assembly area, and a base spares area, all of which were surrounded by a parallel series of four security fences. Each fence was eight feet high with six strands of barbed wire on two outriggers (three on each side). The third fence was electrified with enough voltage to subdue or even kill an intruder.

David King of Limestone narrated the a 2015 tour of the weapons storage area. "I have only gotten used to talking about it in the past ten years," he said, as the bus passed the earth-covered igloos and vaults encased in concrete that once held components of the nation's nuclear arsenal. When King was a member of the security police squadron at Loring in the 1960s, he was limited to one official response to questions about the area. He could "neither confirm nor deny" that it contained nuclear weapons.

The 400-acre site is now part of the Aroostook National Wildlife Refuge maintained by the US Fish and Wildlife Service. Betty Rinehart of Caribou, president of the Friends of Aroostook National Wildlife Refuge, joined King in narrating the tour.

"I represent the past," he said, "and Betty can tell you about the present and the future." As the bus traveled from the Refuge visitors' center toward the storage area, Rinehart said they were on a road that traversed a nesting area for the upland sandpiper. The Friends group arranged for construction of a new route to the weapons area, so the sandpipers can nest in peace.

Such projects support the Friends' goal of restoring the ecological diversity of the area. As a pleasing bonus, when workers tore up an abandoned parking lot to acquire materials for the new road, they discovered a wetland underneath, so another feature of the landscape also is recovering.

The bus rolled slowly past the first of two gates at the entrance to what was the high-security section of the site.

"We called this the 'Sally port,'" King said, describing how a vehicle would be contained between two closed gates while guards at the gatehouse processed the individuals in the vehicle. "You had to pass security to be given an exchange badge," he said, recalling an elaborate system of badges used to establish positive identification for admission to the storage area.

King said the site was independent of Loring Air Force Base—a separate microcosm of the base—and "ninety to ninety-five percent of the people stationed at Loring did not come out here." He said the weapons were transported by trailer to the flight line and then lifted into the aircraft.

"The haul road to the flight line used to be as smooth as a baby's butt," he said as the bus passed the now overgrown roadway. He said grass on the storage site was mown close to the ground to enable guards to see intruders, and at night, "the area was fully lit up like a baseball stadium." A passenger on the bus who also had worked at Loring recalled, "People on the flight line thought the lights were the town of Limestone." Another passenger voiced a common observation: "People lived here all their lives and never knew this was here."

Garbinski offers a response in the introduction to his book: "Although the Cold War can be described as a war of ideology, the truth is that it was also a war of secrets. Secrets kept from the enemy; secrets kept from the American people as well." He dedicates his work to the "Silent Peacekeepers"—military personnel responsible for "secrets kept at the highest level of our military and of our government . . . secrets that had to be kept because they pertained to the most devastating weapons mankind had ever developed."

Today, nature is reclaiming the now decontaminated North River Depot with help from the Friends of Aroostook National Wildlife Refuge — an effort called "From Bombs to Biodiversity." As the fences come down, diverse forms of wildlife are rediscovering the area, causing Rinehart to observe, "This was their territory before the military took over."

Deep Roots

Heritage Envy

Living in Aroostook County has given me a kind of heritage envy. I am sure my ancestors had compelling narratives of the hardships they endured in coming to a strange land, but they arrived so long ago their stories have been lost.

Descendants of immigrants to Northern Maine and adjacent New Brunswick, however, know their roots, especially the Acadians and the Swedes. Tales of their migrations to the region are told and retold, strengthening cultural heritage with each retelling, affirming for each family and individual an identity in their ethnic history.

My sense of separateness resurfaced when I read in a brochure that I was scheduled to talk to a downstate historical society about growing up in a Swedish community. This came as a surprise, since I grew up in a nonethnic suburb of Battle Creek, Michigan.

But there it was in print for all to anticipate. Maybe I could pull it off. Certainly, I masqueraded as a Swede at many a *Midsommar* festival during the ten years I lived in Westmanland (a "suburb" of New Sweden), dancing in traditional costume and helping serve at smorgasbords. Maybe I should talk about how I became a pseudo-Swede. Perhaps I could interview people who did grow up in a Swedish community or relate all I learned about Maine's Swedish history after I was welcomed into their community as a transplant.

I masqueraded as a Swede at *Midsommar* festivals in New Sweden. Photo by Kristine Bondeson, 1998.

Weighing these options caused me to reflect on how I became aware of cultural heritage and how I came to appreciate its connection to a country. I knew all of my ancestors were from England, but our family traditions had nothing to do with our British roots. When I married a second-generation Swede, I became part of a family that celebrated its cultural heritage with foods, language, decor, stories, dances, clothing and personal characteristics similar to those of the Norwegians portrayed on "A Prairie Home Companion."

I didn't even know that the endings "-son" and "-sen" on Scandinavian names differentiated Swedes from Danes. Yet, whenever we moved to a new place and needed professional services, such as a doctor or dentist, my husband would look for Swedish names in the phonebook. He could trust a Swede.

Then we went to Sweden and experienced the homogeneity of an entire country steeped in the same traditions. The idea of a melting pot took on new meaning when we returned to the diversity of the United States, landing in New York where we were dazzled by restaurants, churches, markets and languages of dozens of countries all in one place—all on one street!

Several years later, when we wanted a more rural lifestyle than we had in Concord, New Hampshire, we decided to move to the Swedish colony in Northern Maine. The people of New Sweden, Stockholm, and Westmanland welcomed us warmly, dispelling our fears of being "from away." They seemed genuinely pleased that we were willing to take on the task of restoring an old farmhouse originally built by Swedish immigrants. They even said our interest in their culture renewed their own interest and pride.

Northern Maine's Swedish colony has one of the most well-documented migrant histories in the state, beautifully portrayed in the New Sweden Historical Museum. Residents celebrate not only the annual *Midsommar* festival in June, but also the anniversary of the colony's founding in July, the pre-Christmas *Santa Lucia* festival in December and *Julotta* on Christmas morning.

These celebrations continually renew the history of the Maine colony and the traditions of the old country, educating all generations of Swedes and non-Swedes. To live in the community is to know something about Swedish culture.

I was proud to don the costume of the Swedish province for which Westmanland was named. I loved learning and performing traditional dances and speaking what few Swedish words I could with those who understood them.

During our years in Westmanland, we could hear Swedish spoken on our eight-party telephone line. Residents who could speak the language fluently offered to teach those who wanted to learn or be refreshed. Swedish linguists once came to New Sweden to study the language in Maine because it retained ancient dialects erased by mass communication in the old country.

Every newspaper and magazine article I wrote about the community deepened my appreciation of the fifty-one men, women and children recruited by Maine Commissioner of Immigration William Widgery Thomas of Portland to leave their homeland in 1870 and pay their own passage into an unknown future in Northern Maine. Thomas had served in Sweden as war consul under President Abraham Lincoln. He knew the language and believed the hardy Swedes were well-suited to fulfill his dream for populating the north country.

Thomas called the first settlers *mina barn I skogen* (my children in the woods). Many of their descendants still live in the community. And people who move into the colony as we did come to identify with its unique history as a nineteenth century intentional community.

So, while I couldn't tell the historical society about growing up in a Swedish community, I could certainly describe growing into one. And if anyone thinks I am really Swedish, I'd consider it a compliment.

FEELING ACADIAN

I thought I understood what it means to be Acadian, but celebrating the World Acadian Congress (*Congrès Mondial Acadien*) with the town of Van Buren in 2014 moved my understanding from the intellectual to the emotional and spiritual.

Celebrated every five years in French-speaking countries around the world, the 2014 Acadian Congress was the first to be hosted by two countries—Canada and the United States—through collaboration by the provinces of Quebec and New Brunswick with the state of Maine. Organizers defined the host region as Acadia of the Lands and Forests/*L 'Acadie des terres et forets,* symbolizing the coherence of communities in southeastern Quebec and those in the St. John River Valley of Northern Maine and northwestern New Brunswick.

I had read about the deportation and migration of Acadian people from Nova Scotia to Maine, Louisiana, and New Brunswick in the 1700s. I had visited Grand Pre, Nova Scotia, where Acadians were banished from their homes by the British in 1755. I often visit the site beside the St. John River in Madawaska commemorating both the landing of Acadians in Northern Maine and the annual reunions of families descended from the original settlers.

I have enjoyed Acadian music and theater at the *Musée Culturel du Mont-Carmel* in Lille and the University of Maine at Fort Kent. I have attended Acadian festivals in Madawaska and published dozens of stories celebrating Acadian culture written by and about people from the St. John Valley in *Echoes* magazine.

But I really got the feeling of being Acadian when townspeople in Van Buren adopted me for their celebration of the international 2014 *Congrès Mondial Acadien*.

I could feel the pride among the hundreds of people gathered at Van Buren High School to start the week-long festival, viewing the opening ceremonies live-streamed from Quebec. I was welcomed to a table by women eager to share their secrets for variations on the ployes and *créton* included among the offerings for our hearty breakfast.

Throughout the hall, people who had been punished for speaking French as children spoke their language freely and sang French songs joyfully. I learned the notes, if not the words, of *"C'est le temps,"* written by Van Buren natives Mike and Pat Ezzy, which would become the theme song of Van Buren's Acadian celebration.

Music brought people together again Sunday for a bilingual Mass and concert by the combined choirs of Van Buren and the New Brunswick towns of Saint-Leonard and Sainte-Anne. Every seat was filled in the Romanesque sanctuary of St. Bruno Church as singing rang out from the choir loft high above the congregation: *"Evangeline," "Frere Jacques," "Allouette," "Veillee Rustique"* and other songs accompanied by organ, violin, guitar, tambour, harmonica, clarinet, and flute. Parishioners joined in familiar refrains, especially *"C'est le temps."*

I was seated next to three women attending the Forest family reunion. Symbolically, they were from Nova Scotia, Louisiana and Chicago.

"Like Acadians in 1755, refugees today—2014—are being persecuted on a mountain in Iraq," said the Reverend Jacques LaPointe in opening remarks dedicating the service to refugees around the world. "We were supposed to disappear, but we survived because we reached

Lydia Martin and Pat Ezzy lead Van Buren's *Tintamarre* down Main Street to the international bridge to St. Leonard, New Brunswick during the World Acadian Congress in 2014.

out to others." LaPointe expressed hope that sometime in the future today's refugees would be able to celebrate their survival with festivities like the World Acadian Congress.

To proclaim their survival, Acadians make noise. They call it a *Tintamarre* and march together banging pans, blowing horns, and sounding every kind of noise-maker available to say, "We are here."

I was swept into Van Buren's *Tintamarre*, led by local coordinators Lydia Martin and Pat Ezzy. Down Main Street and across the international bridge from Van Buren to St. Leonard, New Brunswick, we marched, greeted in Canada by a cheering crowd and border officials. Like Mainers, New Brunswickers were decked out in red, white, blue and yellow. They blended together, and that was the point.

Before 1842, St. Leonard and Van Buren were *La Grande Rivière*, one community that spanned the St. John River. The river unified the people on its shores. Family farms extended from one side to the other. Even though the Webster-Ashburton Treaty made the river the boundary between Maine and Canada, the two towns retained a sense of community.

"Everything that has been done to divide *La Grande Rivière* has been artificial, so it hasn't worked," said LaPointe in 1989, when the settlement celebrated its bicentennial with a *Festival des deux rives*. "Even after two hundred years, St. Leonard and Van Buren may be two towns, but they are still one community."

The same spirit existed twenty-five years later, symbolized in an international tug-of-war across the St. John River duplicating a contest held in 1989. Crowds on both sides of the river urged their teams to "Pull! Pull!" until one team was pulled beyond a white line on the grass. The headline on a *Bangor Daily News* photo of the event captured its essence: "Tugging a Tie that Binds Maine, Canada."

The bond between Van Buren and St. Leonard was extended for the Acadian Congress to include two communities in Quebec. Residents of Pohénégamook and St. Athanase, became honorary citizens of Grande Rivière and the four towns celebrated the closing of the Congress together.

I was there because townspeople continued to reach out to me, demonstrating the generosity that meant survival for Acadians in the 1700s. I will never be able to claim Acadian heritage, but I feel its strength, rooted in a history of persecution, throughout the St. John Valley.

I, too, hope that the suffering of the world's refugees will end with a *Tintamarre*.

THE ROCKING CHAIR

"OK. Today is the day I get rid of that old rocking chair," I told myself one crisp, sunny morning near the end of March.

A month ago, I had moved the relic from the bedroom to the center of the kitchen, hoping I would be forced to decide its fate by stumbling around it. Instead, I moved it to a corner of the dining room, less an obstacle, but still out of place. There it sat until, anticipating house guests, my resolve to give it a new home resurfaced.

I bought it years ago at Caribou's famed Second Hand Rose, a consignment shop started by Dot McDuffie in 1987 that became a fixture in the center of town. Even among the fairly eclectic furnishings of my house, the ornate Victorian rocker was an anomaly, and its broken arm swung away from the screw that was supposed to attach it to the chair's back.

My purchase was an act of historic preservation. Dot knew my weakness. She would call me when she acquired an item significant in the history of Caribou. The first time, she had a desk and chair from the Maine Senate that were given to former Maine Sen. Ezra James Briggs of Caribou when the Senate chamber was refurnished.

"I just know it will go downstate," she said, recalling sharp-eyed dealers who snatched up antiques they spotted on visits to her store. "These pieces should stay in Caribou. Don't you think?" Of course, I agreed, and moved the mahogany desk and matching chair with green velvet upholstery into my bedroom.

The rocking chair had belonged to another Caribou legislator, Philip Peterson, who, along with Briggs, was instrumental in restoring Atlantic salmon to the Aroostook River by advocating legislation to improve water quality during the 1960s.

I had been able to return the Briggs furniture to the family, but that option did not exist for the Peterson rocker. I tried to give it back to the new owner of Second Hand Rose.

"If it is broken, I can't sell it," she said. So, it remained in my dining room.

My difficulty in disposing of this chair is a symptom of a general inability to part with old things. It is a fault I am trying to correct, so I loaded the chair into the back of my station wagon and headed for Catholic Charities.

As I neared my destination, I realized I was giving away history. Whoever gets this rocker needs to know about Phil Peterson and what he did for Caribou and Maine. Catholic Charities is a wonderful place to recycle old things, but I drove right by it and returned home with the chair still in the back of the car.

I called Dot McDuffie for the name of someone in the Caribou Historical Society who might have an interest in my treasure.

"I think you should talk to Joe Bouchard," she was quick to respond. So I called Joe, explained my situation and offered to drive the chair over to his home so he could have a look.

"Yes, it's a nice old chair," he agreed, when I lifted the hatch. "You know, there is someone at the museum right now who makes decisions about these things. Why don't you drive out there, and maybe they will take it off your hands."

I was exuberant. And I was welcomed warmly as I entered the museum announcing, "I come bearing an historic chair." And, yes,

Dennis Harris and Dick Cilley knew of Phil Peterson, as well as Jim Briggs.

"We have a fish caught by Briggs right here," Harris said, leading me to a mounted Atlantic salmon.

I carted the chair up the ramp into the back door of the building and offered to carry it downstairs.

"No, just leave it right here in the kitchen," they said. (Déjà vu?) They fiddled with the broken arm and mentioned there were other pieces in the museum bearing warning signs about their fragility.

They asked about the four circular depressions in the amber upholstery of the chair seat and I had to confess they were from an old manual typewriter I had purchased at a church sale in Fort Fairfield because it belonged to a niece of former Maine Gov. John Reed. The heavy black Royal had rested in the chair until I returned it to the family last fall, leaving a permanent decorative detail on the chair cushion.

"I guess I am some kind of reservoir for items of local historical interest," I commented, as I filled out the museum's accession agreement.

I drove home thinking about what makes an item valuable, appreciating that a chair, or desk or typewriter can trigger a host of recollections about an individual's life and accomplishments.

But I am still a long way from discarding stacks of *Maine Times, Aroostook Republicans,* and copies of *Blair and Ketchum's Country Journal* dating back to the 1970s.

EARTH AND ASPHALT

It's lunch time at the hotel in Fort Kent. People sit at separate tables, but they engage in one conversation.

Table 1: "We've been in New Britain now for almost thirty years, but we've got a little piece of land up here we're going to build on."

Table 2: "We moved back fifteen years ago, and we've never been sorry one day since."

The comments echo the letters *Echoes* magazine receives from readers:

"My plans are certainly to return to Maine, if not today, definitely someday to enjoy retirement." *(Nancy Morrow, New Caney Texas.)*

"Although we have lived in many different states, we have managed to make it home to Aroostook County every single summer for almost fifty years, now." *(Saul and Pat Levasseur, Westfield, Mass.)*

"We lived in Caribou for over thirty years. My husband is a Maine native and I grew to love Caribou and enjoy going back every summer for a vacation." *(Ruth Burgess, Hendersonville, N.C.)*

"We return to Maine each summer. Maine, particularly Aroostook County, is a nice place to be from and return to. I haven't forgotten where my roots are." *(Alta Joslyn, Wolcott, Conn.)*

People come back to Northern Maine. What draws them?

Novelist Cathie Pelletier describes a time when she lived in Tennessee and was on her way home to visit her parents in Allagash. She was to pick up a rental car at the airport in Frenchville for the forty-five-mile drive up the St. John River to her family home. When she landed in Frenchville, she was handed a message from her parents. Embedded in that message was the core of Cathie's culture as a native of the St. John Valley. *"Come home quickly. The ice is running."*

The words evoked in her a host of recollections, experiences, images and feelings associated with ice-out on the St. John River. If Cathie broke the speed limit on Route 1 as she raced north to see the ice crash past her house, she was responding to the impact of a tradition that goes back generations in the history of her family, her town, her region.

Ice-out connects her to her ancestors who settled on the banks of the river and to the history of long log drives when men rode down the river with the timber in the spring after spending the winter in the woods cutting trees. "The ice is running" means something special to someone who grows up on the banks of a river.

It represents a culture, passed from generation to generation, that holds people together forever. Whether it's logging, or farming, or fishing, people whose culture is rooted in nature have a confidence that home will always be there, no matter where they go in life. The ice runs every spring.

The first definition of the word "culture" in my dictionary is "cultivation of the soil." It says nothing of concerts, plays or art galleries. It focuses on the process of producing and improving plants and animals. The culture of a particular plant is the method used to grow it—the conditions required: soil type, amount of rainfall, temperature, and climate; space between rows and between plants. People also grow from the ways they interact with their environments.

"It's the dynamics of the experience that determine the degree of rootedness that makes 'home' a reality," says artist and writer Gordon

Hammond, who grew up on Long Island, New York, and relocated to Northern Maine. "The ice running on the St. John in the spring has a direct effect on the people of Allagash. Their lives are shaped and determined by that experience. They *are* the ice running in the spring."

For Gordon, the dynamics of the experience had less to do with the events of nature and more to do with human events: playing stickball on a dead-end street, a secret clubhouse in an abandoned building, a robbery in the neighborhood, a block party, the Dodgers winning the pennant.

"It's a culture too," he says. "It's how people grow—it's the space between rows, the space between people. . . But because the environment is different, the result is different—people come out different, somewhat like the difference between earth and asphalt, trees and brick buildings, rushing spring freshets and opened fire hydrants."

When Gordon went back to Long Island, he couldn't find his home. The landmarks were gone. Shopping malls and insurance companies had filled the open spaces. Streets had been moved and new skyscrapers transformed the downtown into a place he didn't recognize. He traveled back and forth, looking for the turn that would take him to his house. Finally, he spotted one dwarfed building that remained the same and provided orientation.

The country and the city are the "soils" for two different cultures. They produce two different experiences of home. And the experience of going home is the difference between searching for a street in an unfamiliar city and racing up Route 1 to watch the ice run on the St. John.

Gordon and Cathie both have roots. Yet the difference rests in whether, toward the end of life, Gordon will be as drawn to Long

Island as Cathie will be drawn to Allagash. "Depends on the depth of the roots," says Gordon, "whether roots go deeper in earth or asphalt."

Aroostook Ties Run Deep

Aroostook County residents often lament the departure of The County's sons and daughters. Perhaps these woes are short-sighted. People like Francis Malcolm and Mary Barton Akeley Smith demonstrate that out-migration can have a silver lining.

Back in the 1980s, townspeople in Easton were surprised by a sizable gift and plan for creation of an educational science center in their town. Born in 1894, Francis Malcolm never forgot his youth on the family farm located where the town of Easton meets Fort Fairfield. A product of Easton elementary and secondary schools, he earned a bachelor's degree at Ricker Classical Institute in Houlton, Maine, a master's at Cornell and did advanced study at Columbia in preparation for a career in educational administration.

Late in his career, Malcolm invested in real estate in California where he had vacationed and eventually retired. This investment grew and after he died in 1977 Francis Malcolm's memory and his fondness for Aroostook became tangible in the Francis Malcolm Science Center on Route 1A in Easton. His will provided not only funding and four hundred acres of land for construction of the center, but also a vision for its administration and management.

The center offers a variety of natural science and planetarium programs for students and adults: recreation, business and church groups, Scouts, 4-H troops, the elderly, people with disabilities and local clubs. The center welcomes 5,500 to 6,000 visitors each year at no charge for programs and use of extensive nature trails. Through his gift to his hometown, Francis Malcolm enabled future generations to share his appreciation of the natural world.

That same spirit of generosity and love of Aroostook County was expressed by a Presque Isle native who, like Malcolm, also made her home in California. With gifts to both the Mark and Emily Turner Memorial Library and Northern Maine Community College, Mary Barton Akeley Smith has honored her parents, Robert V. Akeley and Hope Greenlaw Akeley, and her late husband Rodney Smith, who came from modest means in England to achieve great success in the electronics industry in California's Silicon Valley.

"My husband came from an environment where he could never have dreamed of achieving the heights of success that he realized in his lifetime. This might be true of many of the students who begin the journey toward achieving their life's dreams by attending Northern Maine Community College," Smith said in a statement read on the occasion of her $1.2 million gift to the college in January 2011.

"Rodney was a philanthropist who believed very strongly in giving to those less fortunate who were working to better their lives and those of their families and communities. He also respected greatly the fact that I loved the area of Northern Maine where my roots are. That is why I believe strongly in the work of the college and want to support its efforts in improving the lives of people and the economy of the region, while paying tribute to Rodney's amazing life in a meaningful way."

The parallels between her husband's life and the lives of working-class students at NMCC were cited when NMCC announced her gift of $5 million in 2012, the largest private donation to any community college in Maine. The donation honored her husband, with creation of the Rodney Smith Center for Fitness and Occupational Wellness, and her parents with conversion of the gymnasium into the Akeley Student Center.

NMCC used funds previously awarded by Smith to establish the Northern Maine Center for Excellence in Alternative Energy Training and Education, a project that allowed for expansion of the college's wind power technology program. In 2010, Smith also honored her parents with a $1 million gift to the Mark and Emily Turner Memorial Library in Presque Isle to create the Robert and Hope Akeley Memorial Wing.

Born in Presque Isle, where she spent her early childhood, Smith moved to Maryland with her parents when her father accepted a position with the US Department of Agriculture. She later met and married Rodney Smith and the couple made a life together in California.

A native of Oldham, England, Rodney Smith grew up in a poor working-class neighborhood, attended an Anglican school and received a scholarship to an exclusive private school. He achieved academically, but socially he felt out of place among the wealthy upper-class students. He left the school at age 16 and enlisted in the British Army and received a degree in electrical engineering.

He left the army at age twenty-seven and migrated to the United States, where he worked a short time for General Electric on the east coast, then spent thirteen years with Fairchild Semiconductor in California, becoming general manager of the company's second-largest division. In 1983, the founders of Altera Corp. hired him as the firm's first CEO and he led the company to great success for two decades before retiring in 2001.

NMCC President Timothy Crowley said Smith's gift will have an economic impact on Aroostook County not only in creating jobs in the short term but also in creating a healthier and more competitive work force long term. "Mrs. Smith shares our vision and commitment to the people of Aroostook County," he said.

Francis Malcolm and Mary Akeley Smith exemplify the generosity of many Aroostook County natives who give back to their communities in countless ways, even if they move away.

HELPING THE FARMER

Six University of Maine seniors sat around a picnic table the week before their 1994 graduation reflecting on how growing up in Aroostook County had influenced their lives.

Celina was from Frenchville, Karen and Paula were from Fort Kent, and Jill was from Fort Fairfield. Angela grew up in Presque Isle, the daughter of an Air Force family, and Holly's family had moved to Limestone with the Air Force the year she entered the University of Maine, so Aroostook had been a home to visit for four years.

Discussion focused on potato harvest and the familiar memories of picking potatoes or working on a harvester, or both.

"Getting up at 4:30 in the morning."

"Going to bed and hearing the tractors."

"And you see the rows . . ."

"And you just close your eyes and your mother is calling you to get up."

"And you get dirty. Holy . . ."

"My fingernails looked like a werewolf's."

"Did you wear rubber gloves and they'd get caught and stretch out and snap back?"

"Yes, my mother taught me that—rubber gloves over your cloth gloves because the cloth got so wet, and sometimes they'd get caught in the rack."

The six young women remembered the hard work that nobody questioned because it was a way of life that involved the whole community. It was work everyone did out of respect and appreciation for the farmer.

"Did your back bother you, working on the harvester? Mine did."

"My father would come home and sleep on the floor. My brother would come in and my father would be lying on the floor like he'd had a heart attack, but it was just his back bothered him so much riding the tractor all the time."

"I remember the farmer I worked for always had to watch the rows and I felt bad for that man, his neck must have hurt so bad. Can you imagine doing that for thirteen hours? He worked hard and worked us hard."

"I remember every harvest saying 'I'm quitting. I can't go tomorrow, Mum, I just can't.'"

"It was dirt pay, you know, thirteen-hour days. It seems like a lot of money when you're in high school. 'Oh. Wow, $400,' but for three weeks of slavery!"

"It was the greatest thing because we would make our own money."

"I remember after harvest going down to Bangor to shop. Everybody would go."

One recollection led to another, mixed with laughter and recognition of common experiences. But the tone of the conversation changed with thoughts that younger brothers and sisters at home might not participate in harvests of the future. Most Aroostook County school districts had discontinued the three-week harvest recess for elementary students and others were considering eliminating the recess for high schools as well.

"It's kind of sad to see it go; you feel like kids are missing something. They're just like everybody else now, like kids from Portland or Bangor. County kids are special because they've had the experience of hard work; they've been initiated."

"People in the County really work hard. Everybody just works and works and works for what they get, and when they get down here (the University of Maine in Orono) it shows. When I've applied for jobs, I've had people see I'm from the County and say, 'Did you work in a potato house?' and when I say, 'Yes,' they say, 'Really? You must be a hard worker.' I've had people say that to me."

"Me, too. And it's too bad, because those kids up there now are not going to have that reputation. They might not become as hard-working and understand the value of money and what it takes to work to get what you want. You may not think that when you're doing it, but eventually you do."

"You appreciate what you have."

"And the job that you're doing. I work in a coffee shop and a lot of people say, 'Oh, this is a dumb job, the most menial job I could ever have, as low as I could get.' But I say, 'Hey, this is better than working on a harvester. I've done a lot worse than this.'"

"You take pride in your work, even if it's flipping burgers."

"Exactly. Working on a harvester, you say, 'I'm going to get all those rotten potatoes out of there.'"

Asked to explain this pride in even a menial task, they remembered the community spirit of harvest.

"The whole community comes together."

"You realize that's how farmers are making a living and you have a part in that. You don't want to let them down."

"A lot of it is families. You appreciate the elders and you learn to respect them."

"Thirteen hours a day for three weeks, you really get silly by about ten o'clock at night. These were kids I would never hang out with in high school, but when I'd see them, it was like we knew something of each other. It was really fun, and I'd miss them."

"Where I worked there was usually at least one person who was another generation, and by the end of it they weren't like somebody's mother any more."

"Last year was the first year my mother hadn't gone in thirty years. It was kind of her get-away. She'd earn some Christmas money or something. And my father takes two weeks' vacation in the fall to drive a harvester for someone, because farming is in your blood. I think once you're a farmer, you're always a farmer."

"Yes and no. Some of them just really want to get away from it, but they're stuck. They have to work."

"It's a hard life. It really is. They work all the time. Work, work, work. They can't make a living, but they're working more than anybody else. But they love it, I guess."

Celina, Karen, Paula, Jill, Angie, and Holly recognized that the values born of their harvest experiences are rare in America today: work hard because you know and care about your employers; take pride in your work because your reputation depends on it. What they brought from Aroostook County to the University of Maine they will take with them wherever they go after graduation. They will tell their children about working together with people of all ages and income levels in a community where everyone was involved in the life of the farmer.

A SENSE OF COMMUNITY

When I first moved to Northern Maine in 1974 I was intrigued by the number of people who had returned after living elsewhere—men and women who had retired here, taken mid-career pay cuts to work here, and people who came because their ancestors settled here a generation or two earlier. And I met young people who returned after graduating from college.

My curiosity inspired a column of profiles for Caribou's weekly newspaper titled "They Came Back." Each story was different, but common themes emerged. People returned to Aroostook County for the pace of life, closeness to nature, and, most frequently, the genuineness of the people. Many returnees felt close to their roots. One could still talk to residents who had known the region's original settlers. Young people knew the stories of how and why their ancestors had come from Sweden, Scotland, Lebanon, Canada, and France to make new homes in Maine.

I found in Northern Maine a culture similar to that which built this country. Aroostook County had retained qualities that once characterized the entire nation when agriculture drove its economy and people were inherently self-reliant. My neighbors remembered days when families provided for most of their needs and bartered homemade goods for things they could not produce themselves. Acquiring money was not as important as being productive, and many families had been relatively unaffected by the Great Depression of the 1930s. "Waste not, want not" was a way of life.

Later they would be told they were "poor" by those who measured wealth in dollars and acquisitions. They would learn to look outside themselves and their communities for prosperity instead of drawing on their own personal and natural resources for strength and survival. Agriculture began to decline, and independence was eroded. Construction of an air force base in Limestone in the 1950s drew people away from the hard work and risk of farming to better paying jobs with pensions. The purpose of farming changed from sustaining families and communities to providing cash income.

Potato farmers were encouraged to increase production to feed people in distant places. Inexperienced in marketing on a national scale, they depended on local brokers and remote buyers to sell their fresh crop, and on local processors to buy potatoes for canned and frozen products and starch. Demands for high yields required new and expensive equipment and loans for financing. When overproduction pushed the price of potatoes below the cost of producing them, the farmer had to learn to look to the federal government for assistance.

The need to stay ahead of debts and meet market demands superseded the need to take care of the land for future generations. Soil eroded, and organic matter disappeared, as expensive fertilizers, pesticides, and herbicides were used to maintain production. Family farms that could not keep up were bought by large corporations for which future generations were nonexistent and volume production was the goal. Farmers even began to call themselves "producers" and "growers" instead of "farmers."

People in rural communities came to believe that ideas from outside were better than their own. Architects from someplace else advocated schools with flat roofs that sometimes leaked and collapsed under winter's heavy snows. Urban renewal experts from someplace else convinced towns they could get big federal grants if they would just level those old buildings on Main Street and build modern malls (with flat roofs, of course).

Businesses owned by local people were replaced by franchises owned by national and multinational corporations. A sense of pride and belonging characterized the ribbon-cuttings of the McDonald's, Pizza Huts, and Kentucky Frieds that came to line the highways. Now Northern Maine could identify with urban areas, forgetting that while franchises provided some jobs, profits would leave the community, unlike the profits of locally-owned businesses. The Main Street that had been a cultural, social, and commercial center gave way to malls dedicated only to commercial values.

Yet, despite losses in town and country, Northern Maine is still a place where people know you by name and care about your well-being. More than once I have been flagged down at high speeds on Interstate 95 by Aroostook friends who wanted to catch up in a roadside chat. Aroostook County is still a place where you can leave your keys in the car when you run into the post office, and you don't have to lock your house for every trip to the supermarket. (You should, however, allow an extra half hour to talk to all the friends you will meet.).

The qualities of life that drew people north in the 1970s remain, attracting a new generation of urban refugees seeking a safe, beautiful, rural environment to raise their families. Not necessarily returning natives, these parents in their thirties and forties are listening to those who remember the days before air force bases and shopping malls, when families and communities supported themselves. They are learning traditions of sustainability and passing them on to their children.

It has been said that today's children will be the first generation in American history to have a standard of living lower than that of their parents. It won't hurt them to know how their great-grandparents grew and preserved their own food and lived without waste. It might help them survive.

Dependence can become a way of life for those who look outside themselves, their families, and their communities for wisdom and identity. But throughout what was once rural America, there are those who remember when work was life and when families depended on themselves and the community for their futures. Their self-reliance made them free and their stories hold a message for our future.

CROSS-BORDER FAMILIES

Former Canadian Prime Minister Pierre Elliott Trudeau once said that living next to the United States is like sleeping with an elephant. Fort Kent native Lisa Lavoie, after completing a master's thesis on her borderland community, concluded that the terrorist attacks of September 11, 2001, woke up the elephant.

"Since 9/11, the people living in the Fort Kent-Clair borderlands have experienced a sea change in their habitual and casual border crossing," Lavoie writes. "The United States transformed a border that had been essentially a non-entity for 200 years into a barrier as a response to real or perceived threats to the country after 9/11."

Lavoie's research documents the emergence of a "psychological border" within the communities on either side, coupled with a significant decrease in car traffic passing into Fort Kent from Clair, New Brunswick, since 2001. Yet, even though militarization of the border has altered connections between Fort Kent and Clair, Lavoie found that the affinity of the bi-national towns, rooted in their Acadian and French-Canadian heritage, has endured.

A 1983 graduate of Fort Kent Community High School, Lavoie received a bachelor of arts degree in English with a minor in behavioral science from the University of Maine at Fort Kent (UMFK) in 2007. She had dreamed of earning an advanced degree, but with a full-time job and occasional teaching responsibilities in the arts and sciences division at UMFK, she needed a program she could pursue from a distance.

In 2011, after her daughter had completed her biomedical science degree at the University of New England and entered physician's assistant school, Lavoie thought, "My time has come." She enrolled at the University of Maine in Orono in a master's degree program in interdisciplinary studies with a concentration in Maine studies.

"The opportunity [distance learning] presents for those of us in the north country is amazing," Lavoie said. She took one course per semester beginning in September 2011. After two compressed-video and four online courses, plus four one-on-one directed studies, she devoted the summer of 2014 to interviews and the fall semester to writing.

Lavoie's topic evolved from her perception of the St. John Valley after living six years in Southern Maine.

"I didn't realize how unique we were," she said. At first, she wanted to focus on what it means to be Acadian and French Canadian. Then she expanded her research to include what it means to live on the border. When her adviser, Carol Toner, suggested she incorporate the effects of 9/11 on the communities of Fort Kent and Clair, the topic began to take shape.

"Borders are human constructs. They often don't make any sense, especially the Canadian-American border," Lavoie said, citing the 1842 Webster-Ashburton Treaty that made the St. John River the international boundary.

"An area that was one people was unceremoniously divided, but the people went about their business," she said, describing decades of easy flow back and forth with friendly exchanges at border stations as residents of Fort Kent and Clair maintained family and business relations.

"After 9/11, that came to a grinding halt," she said. Her interviews with townspeople, a retired Customs and Border Protection (CBP) officer, and town managers on both sides of the border led her to conclude that post-9/11 militarization of the United States side of the border has affected the neighboring communities more than the Webster-Ashburton Treaty.

"9/11 has altered relations between Canada and the United States more than anything else in the twentieth century," she said, citing work by historians Victor Konrad and Heather Nichol. "It's not unique to Fort Kent," she added. When she mentions her research topic to Valley residents, the common response is, "Do I have a story for you."

Her own experience returning to the United States, after conducting an interview in New Brunswick last summer, resembled those of others who reported bellicose attitudes, indiscriminate searches, and long waits, as well as the intimidating effects of "immense signage," visible flak jackets and weapons.

"Put it in park," were the first words of the U. S. Customs and Border Protection agent who greeted Lavoie in Fort Kent after her interview with the mayor of Clair. "Pop the trunk," came next. After a cursory search, the rubber-gloved agent returned her passport without a smile.

"It was totally different from Clair," she said, comparing her return to the United States to her earlier crossing into Canada. "I felt as though I had done something wrong."

Such experiences create what researchers call a "psychological border" that prevents people from crossing because of the anxiety and unpredictability associated with the trip, Lavoie wrote. She found tangible evidence of such avoidance in US Bureau of Transportation records showing a gradual decline in the number of passenger cars entering the United States at Fort Kent each year from 300,008 in 2001 to 199,730 in 2013.

Retired CBP officer Bill Melvin attributed the "we're-in-charge-here" attitude to academy training programs. "The officers coming out of the academies post-9/11 were very enthusiastic," he told Lavoie. "They had joined to try to do something and when they came out of the academy, they were prepared to look for the worst in people. Maybe it takes a few years of knowing or dealing with the public to realize these people have legitimate reasons for crossing the border."

He said post-9/11 directives require officers to ask every passenger to state citizenship, even though "you know the people, you know their children, you know their grandchildren, you know their routines . . . you know it's Sunday and they spend Sunday with mémère and they are coming to visit mémère."

Yet, even with challenges imposed at the border, Lavoie affirms that cultural unity spans the St. John River, keeping the borderland communities on both sides connected and close. "We still have a commonality," she said. "It has been altered, but it endures. The French heritage we share is not going to go away soon."

ACADIANS AND SCANDINAVIANS

When Presque Isle native Don Cyr moved to the St. John Valley to teach school in the 1970s, he lived in one of the buildings in the Acadian Village near Van Buren that had been restored for the nation's 1976 bicentennial celebration. The historic Sirois House was heated with wood, and it took four hours for the house to warm up after Don got home from school. He spent that time reading Acadian history.

The more he read, the more he learned about the connections between his own French-Acadian ancestors and those of the Scandinavians, who settled in Northern Maine in the 1870s. "There was a lot of exchange between Scandinavia and France," he observed.

Now the curator of the *Musée Culturel* in the former Notre-Dame-du-Mont-Carmel church in Lille, and a teacher at the University of Maine at Presque Isle and the Maine School of Science and Mathematics in Limestone, Cyr began to make connections between Acadians and Scandinavians when he read about the Viking invasion of Normandy in the late 800s.

"Danish Vikings settled north of the Loire Valley in France where the Acadians are from. Some with Viking blood migrated south," he said, tracing the blond hair and blue eyes of some Acadians to the Vikings who settled in France.

But genes are not the only way Maine's Acadians are connected to their Scandinavian neighbors in Maine's Swedish Colony of New

Sweden, Stockholm, and Westmanland. The other link Cyr discovered is architecture.

One of the most informative books he read beside the woodstove in the Sirois House was *Acadia: The Geography of Early Nova Scotia to 1760* by Andrew Hill Clark, who speculated that the design for early Acadian log homes came from Sweden. Between 1604 and 1630, the Acadians who settled in North America were all men, explorers who intermarried with natives. Families from France started to arrive in North America after 1630, led by Acadia's second governor, Seigneur d'Aulnay, a nephew of Cardinal Richelieu, advisor to the Royal Court of France.

"There is some evidence Seigneur either spoke to Swedes or visited Sweden to learn how to make houses out of logs," Cyr said. Traditional architecture in France was post and beam construction with a mixture of mud and hay called "wattle and daub" between the logs.

D'Aulnay knew his people would face harsh weather in their new home and realized they would have plenty of trees to use for their houses. So he set out to learn how to build houses using all logs instead of the wattle and daub construction.

"It was a small leap from the timber frame to log-over-log construction," Cyr said.

Thus, Acadian log houses were modeled on an early type of Swedish log house made of hand-hewn timbers flat on all four sides. But there is a difference between this design, exemplified by houses in the Acadian Village in Van Buren, and log houses built in Maine's Swedish colony in the 1870s.

Sometime during the 200 years between Seigneur d'Aulnay's architectural research and the migration of Swedes to Maine, the Swedes modified their log construction. In order to make a tighter seal, more resistant to wind and weather, log houses constructed in New Sweden used logs rounded on the top and concave on the bottom.

"Acadians didn't know about the change," Cyr said. Logs in Acadian houses are flat on all four sides. So if you want to distinguish an Acadian log house from a Swedish one, just examine how the logs fit together.

County
People

THE KIDNEYS LOVED THE
ALLAGASH

Dorothy Boone Kidney would have been delighted to know that when the State of Maine acquired a forty-acre site at Lock Dam connecting Chamberlain and Eagle lakes in the Allagash Wilderness Waterway in 2016, the cabin she and her husband had occupied remained pretty much as they had left it.

Dorothy and Milford Kidney spent twenty-eight summers between 1957 and 1985 in a one-room cabin on Chamberlain Lake tending Lock Dam for Bangor Hydro-Electric Company and registering canoeists for the Maine Bureau of Parks and Recreation. A prolific freelance writer for national and regional magazines, Dorothy also wrote three books about their experiences in the Allagash: *Away from It All, A Home in the Wilderness,* and *Wilderness Journal."*

A native of Presque Isle, Dorothy was living in Washburn when we became acquainted in the 1990s, and she became a regular contributor to *Echoes* magazine, which I edited. Her stories were filled with history and poignant anecdotes, especially the tales of those years in the Allagash, years she and Milford cherished.

Dorothy, who died at age eighty-two in 2001, loved to tell the story of how Milford got his job as dam tender. A radio sermon by Dr. Norman Vincent Peale inspired the couple to make separate lists of their personal life goals. When they compared their lists, they discovered they had written exactly the same things, including helping people and being outdoors. Following Dr. Peale's suggestion, they knelt together and prayed for the opportunity to fulfill those goals.

The couple was living in Yarmouth, Maine, where she taught school and he sold business machines. After a fishing trip to Northern Maine, Milford told his wife about a man he had met at Lock Dam, living in a cabin and working for Bangor Hydro-Electric. "That's what I would like to do," he remarked.

Less than a year later, on a business trip to Woodland, they picked up a copy of the *Bangor Daily News* and Dorothy noticed an obituary for a man named Jim Clarkson who seemed to fit the description of the man Milford had met on the fishing trip. Milford assured her that was the man he met the day he followed a stream in the woods and first saw the cabin at Lock Dam. Dorothy encouraged her husband to apply for Clarkson's job.

"The president and office staff at Bangor Hydro-Electric Company knew Milford well," she recalled in 1998 when I visited her in Washburn. "In his neat business suit, he frequently demonstrated and sold business machines at their committee meetings and conferences."

But when he applied for the job as dam-tender, the company president exclaimed in astonishment, "But Mr. Kidney, that's a job for a hermit. That's not a job for you!" Milford returned home very disappointed, but Dorothy was undaunted.

"You weren't dressed for the part," she told him. "Put on your old hunting jacket, your scruffy pants, your worn boots and go again and apply." He did, and they hired him. The couple's prayer was answered.

"The first year we lived at Lock Dam on Chamberlain Lake we registered about 350 canoeists," Dorothy wrote in 1994. "They didn't begin this wilderness journey unprepared. They dressed for it. Felt hats, usually red or green, were a must to protect their heads from intense sun and driving rain. Long-sleeved, flannel or cotton shirts protected them from sunburn and blackfly bites. They wore sturdy, ankle-top, leather boots for walking in the woods and canvas sneakers for wading and guiding canoes in the streams."

Campers in the 1950s could enter the Allagash by one of three routes, Dorothy recalled. Fly in, drive 150 miles through Canada to Churchill Lake, or paddle twenty miles up Chesuncook Lake, then up Cuxabexis Cove, across Umbazooksus Lake, portage through mucky, black-fly infested Mud Pond Carry to Mud Pond, then across Mud Pond, and down a stream to Chamberlain Lake.

"Food was packed in strong wooden boxes with handles for carrying and each box was numbered," she wrote, adding that guides and camp counselors kept lists of the contents for each box, often carrying the ingredients for each meal in a separate box.

"Canoeists made sure before they left home that they had a hatchet, a canteen, nails, a hammer, a flashlight, bandages, a compass, insect repellent, matches, adequate clothing, and a good book to read if they were windbound."

Things began to change after Great Northern Paper Company opened roads creating easier access from Millinocket, Greenville and Ashland. The Allagash region became a state park—the Allagash Wilderness Waterway—in 1966, and the number of people visiting the region increased rapidly.

"By 1985, several thousand canoeists were entering the waterway annually—a far cry from our 350 in 1957," Dorothy wrote, noting that, in 1991, 3,708 people registered at the Chamberlain Bridge checkpoint alone, with a total of 14,851 entering the Waterway.

"Between 1957 and 1985 we met people from all walks of life making the famed Allagash trip—poor people with worn, patched canoes; extremely wealthy people with expensive equipment and a number of hired guides; city people, out-of-state people, people from other countries. All of them shared a love for the outdoors and many of them had one goal: to run the Allagash, which flows northward for ninety-some miles.

"These feelings and desires have not changed," Dorothy observed. "People have a need to live in simplicity, even for a short period of time, among the trees and streams, as did our ancestors. When they realize they have been living too long under the stress of city life, they seek a clearer perspective.

"They come to the Allagash for a close acquaintance with the cry of the loon, the swirl of white water, and the outline of mountains against a blue sky."

FOCUSED ON AROOSTOOK

It has been said if you do what you love, you'll never work a day in your life. While Paul Cyr of Presque Isle has a number of jobs that could be called work, it is his love of photography that frames his daily routine and defines his identity in Aroostook County.

"I didn't expect it to get this big this fast," he said of the hobby that has spawned a website with more than 10,000 images and a Facebook page with thousands of friends. While he sells digital images, calendars, CDs, and some prints, "It's not a big money venture," he says.

Cyr operates sixty-two housing units in Presque Isle and Easton, manufactures a component for snowmobiles, which he has patented, and does earthwork with a large skid steer loader, but it is his love of photography that gets him outside every day between 3:30 and 4 a.m. to observe and record the world around him.

He maintains inventories of images for about thirty customers, including Aroostook County cities, towns, banks, health care facilities and the Northern Maine Development Commission, which regularly use his photographs for their websites, reports and promotional materials.

"I have a picture of the main street of every town in the county," he said, though most of his images are made within ten miles of his home. He calls his website "an online album" where visitors may select from more than fifty categories to view his work.

Born into a large farm family in Hamlin Plantation, Cyr has always awakened early, so it is natural for him to be up at dawn traveling Aroostook roads with his cameras or monitoring the nine sites on his own property where video cameras survey the activities of wildlife. When something of interest appears on one of the nine screens in his office, he grabs a camera and races to the site.

"I don't sit for hours," he said of a common misconception about his ability to capture extraordinary wildlife shots. With careful observations day after day, "you learn the probability for something [to occur] at a given time." The sites on his farm are inhabited by numerous birds and animals.

He did not discard his old film camera when he switched to digital. He uses it as a prop, or sets it up at one of his photo sites so wildlife will become familiar with it. "When birds get used to the old camera, I put out a newer one and use a remote," he explained.

When a curious bear began to fiddle with the old camera, Cyr got a hilarious shot of the bear "taking a picture" of the photographer. "For non-believers," he said, he posted a video of the whole episode on YouTube with the title "State Street Bears."

"There is a decent amount of wildlife" on his farm, he said, and he is proud to have taken an unusual photograph of a barred owl eating a partridge. "The more difficult it is, if I can pull it off, the happier I am." He is particularly pleased with images of eagles and of the northern lights.

Cyr is also well known for photographs of his Amish neighbors in Easton and Fort Fairfield. He recalled his first contact with members of the community. The year Noah Yoder and his family moved to Fort Fairfield from upstate New York (2007), Aroostook County was buried in exceptional quantities of snow. Yoder asked Cyr to take pictures at his Fort Fairfield farm that he could send back to New York as evidence of the weather they were experiencing.

The next spring, Amish farmers were faced with tasks that required the kind of equipment Cyr uses for his earthwork business. They called on him for assistance, he performed the tasks successfully, and the relationship grew.

His respect for their religious belief, prohibiting the making of "a graven image," allowed him to take photographs as long as he did not show their faces. "Some of them don't mind," he said, but he still doesn't photograph faces. When Amish children can't resist looking up when he drifts overhead in a powered parachute, he said, "I can pull back on the zoom."

When asked to name his favorite images, he responds with the first type of photograph he took: farm aerials. It is a genre he still enjoys, shooting from the passenger seat of a powered parachute, a light aircraft propelled by a snowmobile engine. His current aerials include sweeping views of the St. John Valley and of towns throughout the region, as well as individual farms.

Before he moved to Presque Isle from Hamlin in 1976, Cyr took 300 to 400 aerial color photographs of Aroostook County farms. Many of them still hang on the walls of farmhouses in the area.

MUSICAL DREAMS BECOME REALITY

It's no mistake that the word "roots" is central to the name of a Northern Maine music festival founded in 2006 that has drawn musicians from throughout Maine to perform annually in the bandshell at Thomas Park in New Sweden. For founder Travis Cyr, Arootsakoostik fulfills a dream.

Cyr was certain he would have to leave home to be part of the music scene he envisioned for his future, after he graduated from Van Buren High School in 1993. Bands didn't come to play in Northern Maine, and there was "no place where like-minded folks could gather, meet, perform and appreciate each other," he recalled. So he left.

He had a variety of "employment adventures" including jobs as coach, bag-boy, carpet cleaner, painter, farmer, pizza maker, landscaper, bartender, substitute teacher, warehouse worker, big brother and musician. After attending the University of Maine at Farmington for a while he decided to move to Vermont, where he worked at a plant nursery. "It was great, beautiful, honest work," he said, but even though Vermont was a lot like home, it never felt right, so he moved to the greater Portland area.

"I was never a city guy," he said of his reactions to the cars, lights, people and fast pace of life in Portland. "All the noise and none of the beauty, or just a different kind of beauty than my soul requires," he said. "The County was calling me home."

Music filled the bandshell at Thomas Park in New Sweden.

He remembered sitting in his kayak, alone, watching the sun set over Long Lake, and then watching "that same sun rising again through the fog on the water." He remembered "the smell of the trees and the decaying leaves after a rain in early fall, and the night sky, the dust settling, and the stars—oh my, the stars!"

Ultimately, he could not sacrifice "the quiet comfort of Aroostook County—our small towns and way of life"—for the music scene of the city. After a year in Portland, he returned to Aroostook County in 2001. Rather than seeking the arts elsewhere, he decided to nurture the arts at home.

"When Phish, a band I had listened to and admired since my high school days, came to Limestone and put on not one but three amazing cultural, artistic events, well, that gave me hope," Cyr said of the concerts that drew thousands of Phish fans to the former Loring Air Force Base.

Cyr began playing when and wherever he could—in bars, restaurants, living rooms, and art galleries. He wove together the chords and the words he had written over the years, creating a rich repertoire of original songs expressing his love of nature, peace, and solitude. As he played here and there in Maine, he crossed paths with other musicians who inspired him to start the annual music fest in New Sweden.

"I began to realize that there is some incredible music being created and performed right here in our state," he said, adding that many musicians expressed a desire to play in Aroostook County. But where?

Built in 1936, the Thomas Park music bowl has been the stage for Swedish Midsommar festivals, band concerts, church services, Boy Scout programs, and town celebrations for more than seventy-five years. Facing a hillside of outdoor seating, it was the perfect venue.

The festival was launched in the park in September 2006. Called "Gardenstock," the first concert drew about forty people to hear three local singer/songwriters. The event raised about $150 in food and funds to donate to a local soup kitchen.

The next year, they changed the name to Arootsakoostik, fusing the name of the county with acoustic and/or roots music. The second concert featured eight musical acts, doubled the size of the audience, and raised $300 to donate to the Make-A-Wish Foundation of Maine.

"The founders and organizers of this event showed that the true sentiment of Arootsakoostik is giving to others," said David Spooner, a member of the committee that manages the park. Spooner praised the event planners for not only giving the people of Aroostook County "the opportunity to listen to amazing music that originates from around the state of Maine right here in central Aroostook," but also for leaving the park in better condition than they found it. "Not a piece of litter could be found."

When it was evident the aging bandshell required major reinforcement, Arootsakoostik donated $1,000 after the 2012 concert, the largest single donation the park committee had received.

Though many performers were Portland-based, they reflected Cyr's original goal of showcasing people with roots in Aroostook County. Fellow organizer and musician Frank Hopkins of Portland hails from Wallagrass. Lil' Timmy Findlen, originally from Fort Fairfield, with his Aroostook Hillbillies, came from Nashville, Tennessee. The John Clavette Band came from Portland, maintaining its record of performing at every Arootsakoostik since its founding. Clavette is from Madawaska.

"Musicians have told me they look forward to coming to Aroostook," Cyr said. "I am humbled by the number of people offering me their hands," Cyr said, giving special credit to his parents, Rick and Rhonda Cyr, and to his co-organizer and fellow musician Matthew Beaulieu of Van Buren.

"We are just blown away by the support," Cyr said, describing the event as a "family reunion" for participants eager to share their talents without the ego issues one might expect. "They totally get the idea of community. It has taken on a much bigger meaning than anything Matt or I could envision. It warms our souls."

MET SINGER RETURNS TO ROOTS

My spine tingled and my eyes teared as a rich contralto voice filled the sanctuary of Holy Rosary Church in Caribou with "Glory to God" from Handel's Messiah. The occasion was the annual holiday concert of the Caribou Choral Society. The soloist was Teresa Herold of Fort Fairfield, who returned to Aroostook County after seven years singing on the stage of the Metropolitan Opera House in New York City.

Extending her voice into the soprano range for the solo, the deep quality of the contralto resonated without a microphone. "I don't use a mic. It's one hundred percent acoustic sound," she told me, adding that opera singers usually rely on acoustics instead of microphones. She said she learned a lot about projecting her voice by climbing into "the nosebleed section" of the Metropolitan Opera House and observing how singers made their voices "cut through the orchestra."

"The Met seats 3,800 people. That's more than the population of my hometown," she said. Growing up in Fort Fairfield, Teresa heard music every day of the week as her mother, Susan Herold, gave private violin and piano lessons in their home. She became a student on both instruments at age five.

The 1998 Fort Fairfield High School graduate played in school bands and orchestras through the years and performed with the choirs, often as an accompanist. The diversity of her talent was recognized when she was named to three different All-State Music Festival ensembles: orchestra as a freshman playing viola, band as a junior playing flute, and chorus as a senior.

It was not until she was a student at the University of Southern Maine that she took her first voice lesson. She intended to earn a music education degree in flute, but her professors encouraged her to pursue voice, as well. She studied with Ellen Chickering, associate professor of voice, and ended up with a double major in flute and voice music education.

"My first operatic role ever was Cherubino in Mozart's 'The Marriage of Figaro' in 2001 at USM," she said. "It was not only the first time I had been in an opera but was also the first opera I had ever seen live."

After graduation in 2002, she performed in her first young artist program with PORTopera in Portland, as Veronica in Bizet's "Dr. Miracle."Her USM professors also urged her to attend graduate school, and she won a graduate assistantship to Indiana University in Bloomington to study voice performance. Eager to perform, she went from Indiana to Seattle in 2005 where she entered the Seattle Opera Young Artists Program.

Intense training included lessons, coaching, fully staged operas and outreach to schools. Summer training programs took her to the operas of Central City, Colorado; St. Louis, Missouri; and Chautauqua, New York. Other performances included the Bach Festival Chorale in Carmel, California, and the Spoleto Festival USA in Charleston, South Carolina.

Her first attempt to apply for an audition at the Met, while in grad school, had been denied, but the dream eventually became a goal. In 2007, she decided to apply again. This time she was granted an audition. The director of the Lindemann Young Artist Development

Program at the Met had heard her sing in Seattle. Teresa would audition for the program by singing two arias for James Levine, music director of the Metropolitan Opera.

She sang Rossini's "Cruda Sorte" and Handel's "Hence, Iris, Hence Away." She thought she had blown the audition when she received an email afterward saying the young artist role was "not the best next step" for her. Five months later she received an email from Lenore Rosenberg, artistic administrator for the Met, offering her a contract as a cover (understudy) for the main stage in the opera "War and Peace" by Prokofiev.

"An email from Lenore Rosenberg was like Christmas in July," Teresa recalled. "You say a little prayer, then click on it, and your whole life changes for the better." As a cover, she memorized and rehearsed so she could step in for the singer playing two characters in the opera. "We even had our own wigs and costumes created for us, just in case," she recalled.

The show ran fourteen times. Teresa got her chance when the singer for whom she was covering was too ill to perform in the last show. Teresa made her debut at the Met in January 2008 playing Matryoshka and Mavra Kuzminichna in "War and Peace."

"I have never even walked on this stage before in my life, and now I am going to perform on it," she thought at the time. Now she reflects, "I sang all the right notes and acted well enough, and the rest is seven seasons worth of history."

Because it happened overnight, her family was unable to see her first Met performance, but "they made it to all of my other performances and then some. What I did would not have been possible without my family. What I am doing now would not be possible without them, as well as many other friends and colleagues."

After "War and Peace" she auditioned again and was offered her first official and favorite role: Rossweisse in Wagner's "Die Walkure." She performed and/or covered in eleven operas during her seven seasons at the Met. In off-season, she would return to Northern Maine, where she has a home near her family in Fort Fairfield.

"Maine was always refreshing, and I hated to leave," she said. She grew weary of traveling to and from the crowded city and developed a new appreciation of "all that nature has to offer" in Aroostook County. She began thinking about opportunities in Aroostook and finally decided not to return to New York for an eighth season. She moved back to Fort Fairfield and taught K-12 band and chorus for the Van Buren School District. "Here I am challenged in new ways. It's very rewarding."

Outside school, she became involved in Aroostook River Voices, a choral and musical group directed by Larry Hall with members from all over The County and beyond; the University of Maine Presque Isle Community Band with Jon Simonoff; the Northern Maine Chamber Orchestra with Kevin Kinsey; and, of course, the Caribou Choral Society with Daniel Ladner.

"There is so much music to get involved with here, it is definitely not lacking. I am absorbed in Northern Maine."

Skiers Inspire Groomers

Every time I ski on the beautifully groomed trails in Limestone, I tell myself to write a thank you to Norman Page, who maintains the trails at Trafton Lake and at the Aroostook National Wildlife Refuge, on the former Loring Air Force Base. I call him my personal trail groomer because often I am the only one enjoying his freshly set track.

Page is one of a number of people in Aroostook County who volunteer time to give skiers a first-rate experience. Gerry Roy maintains trails in Madawaska, Tom Campbell in Stockholm, the Plourde family in Westmanland, and Linda Milligan and Amanda Barker in Ashland, to name a few.

Supported by donations from their communities and fundraisers—from bottle recycling to spaghetti suppers—to pay for gas and maintenance, groomers seldom detail the number of hours they spend on snowmobiles to make trails, but they all are avid skiers, eager to share and enjoy the fruits of their labors on the trails.

"I like to do it," says Page, who grooms three miles of trails at Trafton Lake and about ten miles at the refuge. "I go when they need it. I've been doing it for thirty years." Page, a retired farmer and master skier, says he is rewarded for his efforts by seeing people get outside. "When I see seven or eight people out there, it makes me want to do more."

Tom Campbell of Stockholm agrees. "The greatest reward for me is seeing the trail beat up," he says. "That's what I do it for." The greatest frustration, in addition to getting stuck, is seeing the trails unused. Campbell, a machinist at Huber Corp. in Easton, grooms the Snowy Mountain Trail behind the former Stockholm Elementary School—now the town office—and a trail near his home, a total of about eight miles. "It's so nice to go out your back door and ski," says Campbell, who made the flat drag, roller and track setter he uses to groom the trails.

After a snowfall, he packs down the trails with the snowmobile, drags them, rolls them—creating a corduroy surface with a comb attached to the roller—then sets the track, covering the trails at least four times. "By Thursday, I try to make sure the tracks are freshened up for the weekend," he says, adding he often works until 9 or 10 p.m. His wife, Donna, says she's a "groomer's widow."

Linda Milligan of Ashland grooms early in the morning for the same reason Campbell grooms late at night: "The trails set up best when it's cold," she says. "I just roll out of bed and put on my layers." She begins grooming between four and five a.m.

A ski coach for Ashland middle and high school students, Milligan grooms about three miles of trails for skate skiing around her home on the Wrightville Road. Her friend Amanda Barker, a forest ranger, grooms four miles of trails with a set track for classic skiing on the farm of Ed and Marilyn Chase on the Garfield Road.

"We hope more people will come out and use these trails, free and open to the public," says Barker, describing a family fun day on the Chase farm. Organizers of Ashland's fun day rent a trailer full of ski equipment from the Maine Winter Sports Center (MWSC), for those who don't have their own gear, and offer participants a hot dog roast, stew, and home-baked treats out on the trail.

Limestone holds a similar winter fun day behind Limestone Community School. Children on sleds and tubes speed down the hill while volunteers outfit people of all ages with skis from the MWSC trailer. Rotary Club members sell hot dogs and buns to be roasted over a fire. Inside, the Fantasyland Cowboy Band provides music in the cafeteria while participants warm up with chili, chicken stew and chocolate brownies a-la-mode.

Elizabeth Pelkey, assistant residential life director at the Maine School of Science and Mathematics (MSSM) in Limestone, appreciates the "sense of community pride" she sees in Aroostook County, especially on the trails. "I had no idea that groomed cross-country ski trails existed for public use until I went to college," she says. "I guess I just thought they were something special for the Olympics and that sort of thing."

A native of Penobscot County (Winn and Mattamiscontis), Pelkey said, "We always had cross-country skis, and my mom would get all excited and want us to go as a family, but my siblings and I hated it with a passion. Cross-country skiing meant trudging through knee-deep snow for hours while we took turns breaking trail, huffing and puffing and sweating to death."

After Pelkey moved to Aroostook County in 2008 to attend Northern Maine Community College, she was invited to join her uncles for a ski on the groomed trails at Caribou High School. "They had to beg me to go and it was bitterly cold, but once I stepped into the track a light turned on and I realized, 'Hey! This is why people like cross-country skiing!'" She skied regularly thereafter and shared her love of cross-country skiing with students at MSSM.

"It's been pretty awesome to have their first experiences on skis be drastically more positive than mine were," she says. "I'm so blessed to live in a community that values keeping active in the winter months. It's nice to have more than one option for outdoor activity when we live in a snowy wonderland."

AROOSTOOK SKIING LEGEND

"First he was a skier."

So began remembrances of an Aroostook County sport legend at a memorial service in New Sweden in 2015. Children and grandchildren of Ralph L. Ostlund, who died at age ninety-two, expressed the thoughts and feelings of many Maine athletes and other friends for whom Ostlund exemplified fitness and friendliness.

Heads nodded when son Jeffrey observed that his father had probably outskied a number of those gathered at Gustaf Adolph Lutheran Church and had danced with more than a few of the ladies.

"He always won his age group until he was the only one in his age group," recalled one of his grandchildren of the man who cross-country skied whenever possible well into his 80s. And when the snow melted, he ran and biked.

"Running and skiing are the best things I ever did," he told me in an interview in 2004, explaining he didn't ski much between his youth and his fifties. "I didn't ski when I was in my prime," he said. "I skied every day after I retired."

Those who knew him might say he reached his prime late in life. Dozens of trophies, medals, ribbons, and plaques, including one for the eighty-five-and-over division, attest to his achievements. When Ralph was eighty, his children gave him two kayaks, one for him and one for a person to accompany him on excursions. At eighty-five, however, Ralph bought a new kayak that gave him more speed.

Ralph Ostlund at the Nordic Hertiage Center, Presque Isle.

Ralph's athletic ability was exceeded only by his capacity for affection. His greeting was a hug, at least for the ladies, and he often expressed his love of family by saying, "I was born into a good family, I married into a good family, and I raised a good family."

In 2012, he told *Bangor Daily News* columnist Robin Clifford Wood, "I'm a rich man without money. Good health, family, what more could you ask for?" He told Wood he still skied at age eighty-nine, "but I can't take hills and corners like I used to." He might well have maintained his agility had he not suffered an unusual, life-threatening illness in April of 2003 that would have killed many eighty-year-olds. He attributed his recovery to his physical fitness.

Ralph also loved to dance, especially the Swedish hop, and often was the last one off the dance floor. He told Wood he sometimes even danced alone. "When it's cold and miserable, there's only so much exercise you can get walking around the house, so I put Swedish music on and dance in the kitchen." When he felt too tired to dance at a recent family wedding, he lamented to his son, "Oh, to be eighty-five again."

Born in 1923, one of eight children, Ralph began skiing as a toddler on wooden skis made by his father. He competed in local cross-country races until he had to quit school in order to work full time. He won most of the races he entered.

"I s'pose I could ski just as soon as I could walk," he told Wood. He grew up during the days of long-distance races between Bangor and Caribou and from town to town in Aroostook County. His brother Buck skied the 179-mile Bangor-to-Caribou marathons in 1936 and 1937, and New Sweden residents were top competitors in winter carnivals organized by Northern Maine communities.

"We had an athletic club and we always had some of the best skiers in the area," Ralph told ski historian Karla Wolters. "New Sweden was proud of their ski team because they won a lot of carnivals and they bought the club white ski suits."

He remembered when "they used to have wide skis and only one pole . . . and then my wife and I skied with the kids for fun. And then I got into racing and waxing."

"It was never about him," Wolters said. "He was a humble person who loved skiing. He wanted everybody to know it is a great sport, and he never turned away anyone who wanted to know about ski history."

New Sweden native Lendal "Lefty" Johnson, who skied thousands of miles with Ralph over the years, echoed Wolters' view. "His big reason for skiing was enjoyment," Johnson said, minimizing the importance of winning.

Ralph got Don Peters of New Sweden hooked on skinny skis and the two logged thousands of miles together. Peters recalled competing with Ralph in the five-mile Henry Anderson Race between Caribou and New Sweden: "Once Ralph led on the straightaway part of the course, I don't think the very best high-school skier could have beaten him."

In nominating Ostlund for the Maine Ski Hall of Fame, Caribou native and avid skier Catherine Brewer called Ralph a local icon who inspired and taught many to ski. "His presence in our ski community has been an important part of its foundation and growth—from small-school winter carnivals and community ski races to hosting World Cup events at our Tenth Mountain and Nordic Heritage Center venues."

"Fifty-mile races were part of his winter lineup," Brewer said, citing the Sam Ouellet races in Ashland requiring skiers to finish twenty-five miles each day of the weekend and to participate for five years in order to earn the race plaque. "Ralph skied the race into his seventies with his friend Lefty."

Ralph's second-youngest grandson, John Ringer, concluded the memorial service by wishing his grandfather "endless ski trails" and promising to follow his advice to do four things: smile and say hello, be active, when you get the chance get up and dance, and love and cherish your family.

A Legend in Lille

We met at the Northern Maine Fair in Presque Isle in July 2014. I was tending a display of magazines in the fair's Historical Pavilion. One copy featured a cover photo of the imposing French Baroque Notre-Dame-du-Mont-Carmel Church in Lille, which is now a cultural museum.

"I can tell you a story about that church," Rita Lannigan of Presque Isle said as she studied the display. Rita's story led me to a series of stories that suggest her grandmother, Alma Dube, was something of a legend in Lille.

When Notre-Dame-du-Mont-Carmel closed its doors in 1978, Alma was its oldest member, Rita told me. "She was devastated. The church was her life—the church and her kids."

The mother of eighteen children, Alma lived near the church and visited daily, sometimes more than once a day. "If we couldn't find Grammy, we'd go across to the church," Rita said, adding that her grandmother would stay all day on holy days of obligation.

Alma was in her nineties when the church closed for lack of funds. She did not have a vehicle to travel to the nearest church, down the road in Grand Isle. To symbolize her mourning, Alma hung a memorial wreath on the locked front door of the church building.

Her gesture caught the attention of a photographer from *National Geographic* on assignment in the St. John Valley for a story about the Madawaska border region encompassing towns in Maine and New

Pastel painting of Alma Dube keeping a vigil in front of her church.

Brunswick on opposite sides of the St. John River. Photographer Cary Wolinsky wanted an image to portray the feelings of parishioners about the closing of their church, according to museum curator Don Cyr of Lille, who remembers the *National Geographic* story.

Alma agreed to pose with her wreath on the steps of *Notre-Dame-du-Mont-Carmel* as though keeping a vigil. The image appeared in the September 1980 edition of *National Geographic*, one of twenty-six photographs illustrating a nineteen-page article by Perry Garfinkel titled "Madawaska: Down East with a French Accent."

A copy of that issue found its way into a doctor's office in the upper peninsula of Michigan, where Rita's sister, Barbara Ouellette of Munising, picked it up while waiting for an appointment. One can only imagine the expressions of others in the waiting room when Barbara recognized her grandmother on Page 400 of the magazine.

"They thought she had lost her loot," Rita recalled. "She was so excited. She asked the doctor if she could buy the magazine, and he gave it to her."

The family was unaware the St. John Valley had been featured in the magazine and that Alma Dube appeared in the article. Barbara called her sister in Presque Isle, and her excitement spread within the family.

"My mother thought it was cool," Rita said, describing the reaction of Aline Dube Willette, Alma's eldest child, when she learned her mother's picture was in the magazine. "The article resulted in a number of family members subscribing."

Rita and Barbara are two of Aline and Wallace Willette's nine children, with dozens of cousins related to the 18 children of Alma and Alfred Dube. Their brother, Gary Willette, was so impressed with his grandmother's photo he commissioned artist Boyd Pryor of Portage Lake to reproduce the image as a pastel, now a precious family heirloom.

After meeting at the fair, Rita and I found copies of the September 1980 *National Geographic* and agreed to get together to continue our conversation. In the meantime, I mentioned our encounter to Don Cyr, who had his own story to tell about Alma Dube.

He was living in the church rectory next door to the church and was among the people interviewed and photographed when *National Geographic* came to the St. John Valley to feature the lives of people living on the international border. He had met Alma and knew of her but did not know her well.

"For some reason, quite a while after the article appeared, I decided to turn on the lights illuminating the statue of Our Lady of Notre Dame in front of the church," Cyr recalled. "I had never had the urge before, but something inspired me to turn on the lights. They stayed on all night."

The next day he discovered his decision might not have been his alone.

"When I went to the post office the next morning, I learned Alma Dube had died during the night. Townspeople were saying she had lit up the church," Cyr said.

"She probably did."

Before She Died,
She Worried about a Pine

I had just packed the last load of stuff into the car before a ten-day trip near the end of April when the phone rang.

"Are you the lady who writes for the newspaper?" the caller asked.

Our chat was animated, but brief, full of facts and family history. She wanted to tell me about a certain tree in Ashland, but I knew there was more to her story. She was the kind of person I wanted to interview in person. She gave me her Caribou address and phone number, and I promised to pay her a visit when I returned.

Two weeks later, back home in Caribou, I was sitting on my front porch reading the newspaper when I had an odd premonition that I was going to recognize a name in the obituaries. I didn't know who it would be, but I slowly paged in from the back of the section, and there she was, tucked into the lower right corner of the page: "Dorothy W. Peterson, 97, died at her home in Caribou on May 10, 2015," with only a list of survivors and the date for her burial (May 23 in Ashland) as additional information.

I felt a sense of loss for a person I did not even know. Or did I?

"They call me 'Dot,'" she had told me. Her name rang a bell. I felt sure we had met during my forty years in Aroostook County, some of them covering Caribou news. My suspicions were confirmed when I learned later of her active participation in community groups, such as Cooperative Extension. Just before her death, she was selling raffle tickets for a quilt she had made and donated to the Advent Church in Limestone to raise money for a handicapped-accessible bathroom.

"I'm under house arrest," she had joked, lamenting limits on her activity after a hospitalization in December.

"I was a Walker from Walker Hill—Dorothy Frances Walker," she had explained, tracing her Ashland roots. And even though her family home had burned years ago, and the property had new owners, a gigantic two-hundred-year-old pine tree remained in what was the yard. Her concern about the future of that tree prompted her call to me on April 27. What would happen to the stately pine?

With the knowledge of her passing, I wondered what she had wanted to tell me and why. I began to think about values and how they change as we age. I reflected on our almost instinctive search for permanence as mortality becomes real. When we approach the end of life, what emerges as important?

"I'm ninety-seven, but I still have all my faculties," Dot asserted in our conversation. It was clear she was correct. I am sure she had no idea that a few days later, May 2, she would suffer from a stroke paralyzing her right side and limiting her ability to communicate.

"Home. Home," was all she could say from her hospital bed, according to her daughter Gretchen Uhas, who welcomed me into her mother's home as the family sorted her belongings. Before she was stricken, Dot had told Gretchen she had contacted me and was looking forward to our visit.

We sat at the kitchen table where Gretchen had been wrapping the contents of her mother's cupboards in newspapers and placing them in boxes. Dot's cat Sally munched over her bowl on the floor beside me, unaware that she would soon have a new home with Dot's son.

What was important about that tree, we asked each other. Dot so worried it would be cut down; she had even made an unsuccessful attempt to buy back the property to preserve it. Gretchen's brother David arrived, then her sister Nadine Moreau.

"All I can remember is that every trip to Grammy's we knew we were almost there when we could see that tree," Gretchen recalled of family trips to the home of Dot's parents, Arthur and Abby Walker. Together the three siblings recalled the drive from Caribou through Washburn and a community they called "Frenchville," past a variety store on the right until, at the top of a huge hill, they could see the tree in Ashland.

"You go down the hill and start up again and it's on the left, past Ellis' farm," David said.

"It's just a pine tree, but it was important to the family," Gretchen said. "It was the last thing about the property that mattered."

And its value magnified when it turned out to be one of the last things that mattered to a person who remembered that the tree was old when she was young and who hoped it would live long after she was gone.

ACKNOWLEDGMENTS

Sincere thanks to those whose contributions are embedded in this collection of stories: Rick Levasseur, editor extraordinaire; Gordon Hammond, inspiration for ideas expressed in *Echoes;* Jenny Radsma, wordsmith extraordinaire; Kristine Bondeson, master proofreader; the people who shared their stories; and the staff at Islandoport Press who breathed life into *True North.*

About the Author

Kathryn Olmstead moved to Northern Maine in 1974, seeking a life close to nature and to people who knew how to derive sustenance from the earth. A Michigan native, she and her New Jersey-born husband Jim Swanson worked to restore an old farmhouse, grow vegetables, heat with wood, and live without plumbing. Those first ten years in Westmanland grounded and shaped her career as a journalist and teacher in Maine. A graduate of the University of Illinois with a master's degree from the University of Wisconsin, she became a correspondent and later a columnist for the *Bangor Daily News,* an editor of Caribou's weekly newspaper, a district representative for US Senator Bill Cohen, and a member of the University of Maine journalism faculty for 25 years, the last six as associate dean in the College of Liberal Arts and Sciences. She was the Maine correspondent for agricultural newspapers in Vermont and Kansas, and contributed to the *Christian Science Monitor, American Journalism Review, USA Today, The World and I, Maine Townsman,* and *Islandport Magazine.* She co-authored a World War II memoir, *Flight to Freedom,* published in 2013, and was inducted into the Maine Press Association Hall of Fame in 2018. She and Long Island, New York-native Gordon Hammond founded the quarterly magazine, *Echoes,* in 1988, which she edited until it closed in 2017. In 2020, the coronavirus pandemic brought her full circle, back to a simpler life in Aroostook County, close to the natural world and the people who share her appreciation of it.